Mori Yōko

Mori Yōko, born in Shizuoka Prefecture in 1940 and a graduate of Tokyo University of Fine Arts and Music, was known for her polished short stories and novellas of life and love among young urbanites until her premature death of cancer in July 1993. She worked at an advertising agency for three years before turning to fiction, and her witty dialogue, quick pacing, and astringent view of life won her popularity among Japanese young women. One selection of short stories, *Bedtime Stories*, is available in English within Japan in the Kodansha English Library series of paperbacks.

Mori also published much non-fiction, including accounts of life with her British husband and their daughters, conversations or linked essays with other authors, and several volumes of independent essays. Her cautionary parable here, presented in a clear and straightforward style but with a bite in the end, was written for a column in a popular magazine for young women.

First published in *AnAn*. Copyright 1991 by Mori Yōko. The essay also appears in the author's book *Hi-jōshiki no bigaku* (Anti–Common Sense). Reprinted by permission of Magazine House and the author's estate.

逃がした魚は大きかった

森　瑤子

由美ちゃんが、大学時代からつき合っていたボーイフレンドと別れて、別の人とお見合いで結婚したのは三年ほど前だった。

元々、恋愛と結婚は別のものと彼女は考えていた。結婚はある意味で家と家との結びつきであり、夫となる相手は世間に出しても恥かしくないような人物でなければならなかった。そして何よりも、物質的に彼女の一生を保障してくれなければ困るのだ。

大恋愛の末に結ばれるわけではないから、アバタもエクボということはありえなかった。先行するの

• *nigashita [nigasu] sakana wa ōkikatta* "the fish that got away (lit., 'the let-get-away fish') was big" • *Yumi-chan ga daigaku-jidai kara tsukiatte [tsukiau] ita bōifurendo to wakarete (wakareru)* "Yumi separated from her college-days boyfriend, and" • *betsu no hito to omiai de kekkon shita* "she married another man through an arranged meeting" • *~no wa san-nen hodo mae datta* "it was three years ago that ~ " • *motomoto* "from the beginning" • *ren'ai to kekkon wa betsu no mono to kanojo wa kangaete (kangaeru) ita* "she believed that love and marriage were different things" • *kekkon wa aru imi de ie to ie to no musubitsuki de ari (de aru)* "marriage is in a sense the linking of two families" • *otto to naru aite wa seken ni dashite (dasu) mo hazukashiku nai yō na jinbutsu de nakereba naranakatta* "the man to become your husband must be a person one is not ashamed of in polite society" • *soshite* "and" • *nani yori mo* "above all (lit., 'even more than anything')" • *busshitsu-teki ni kanojo no isshō o hoshō shite kurenakereba (kureru) komaru no da* "he should be (lit., 'it would not do if he couldn't be') a good provider for her (lit., 'guarantee her life materially') all her life" • *dairen'ai no sue ni musubareru (musubu) wake de wa nai kara* "since they weren't joined (in matrimony) following (lit., 'as a result of') a grand love affair" • *abata mo ekubo to iu koto wa arienakatta (aru)* "it wasn't a matter of blind love" • *senkō*

❖ *nigashita sakana*: *nigasu* and *nogasu* (both meaning "to let get away") are synonymous, but only the former is possible here. Cf. the English, "You should have seen the fish that got away." ❖ *Yumi-chan ga*: The repeated use of the personal name plus the diminutive *-chan* throughout this short essay gives the impression that Yumi is spoiled, coddled, and self-indulgent; basically the author is speaking from a position of authority to someone much younger. ❖ *omiai*: an arranged meeting (usually by relatives or acquaintances) for the purpose of marriage after a period of dating; cf. *ren'ai kekkon* ("love marriage"). ❖ *kangaete ita*: *kangaeru* and *omou* can both be translated as "think," but the former shows more consideration and thus is close to believe. ❖ *otto to naru aite*: here, *to naru* could be replaced by *ni naru*, but the former would seem to broaden the perspective beyond the individual case to matters in general; *aite* (lit., "mutual hand"), someone that one has dealings with as a partner, client, opponent, etc., with no fixed translation. ❖ *seken*: here means "society"; in other contexts "public opinion." *Seken ni dasu* is a fixed phrase, meaning "to send out into society (the world)." ❖ *jinbutsu*: connotes personality, ability, status, and appearance, which are not included in the word *hito*, for example. ❖ *nani yori mo*: a set phrase = "above all," "more than anything else." ❖ *hoshō shite kurenakereba komaru*: the primary meaning of *komaru* can be paraphased as "to not know what to do and be tormented about it; be unable to make a judgement on something, or handle it properly, and agonize over it"; the word has various secondary meanings and usages, all connected with being in trouble, inconvenienced, faced with a problem, embarrassed, at a loss, etc. *-Nakereba* + *komaru* = if you don't do this or that, there is going to be trouble of one sort or another (i.e., you should do ~) ; *-eba* / *-reba* + *komaru* = if you do this, there well be trouble (i.e., you should not do ~). ❖ *abata mo ekubo*: an allusion to a well-known saying, *Horete shimaeba abata mo ekubo* ("If you fall head over heels, even pockmarks are dimples"); i.e., love is blind). ❖ *arienakatta*: *-eru (uru)* / *-enai* can be added to the stem of certain verbs for the meaning "can" / "cannot."

---

suru no wa jōken de aru "her conditions (for a marriage partner) took priority"

は条件である。由美ちゃんは、学歴と収入の高さに
加えて、百八十センチ以上と、背の高いことも、必
須条件に加えた。
愛してもいない男と結婚するという事に関して、
彼女はそれほどの危惧を抱いてはいなかった。どん
な恋愛だって、いずれは冷めるものだ。かつては
熱々だった相手と冷め果てた関係を延々と持続する
ことの方が、寒々しく耐え難いように思われた。
大学生活を通してのボーイフレンドは、最初から
遊びのつもりだったので、たいして波風もたたずに
別れることができた。彼は面白おかしく遊ぶには良
かったが、将来的な出世コースからは外れた若者だ
った。
お見合いの相手は、理想を絵に描いたような男性

• *gakureki to shūnyū no takasa ni kuwaete (kuwaeru)* "in addition to a good (lit., 'high') academic record and income" • *hyakuhachijū-senchi ijō to, se no takai koto mo hissu-jōken ni kuwaeta* "she added being tall—having a height of 180 cm. or more—to her essential conditions" • *aishite (aisuru) mo inai otoko to kekkon suru to iu koto ni kanshite (kansuru)* "as for marrying a man she didn't even love" • *kanojo wa sore hodo no kigu o idaite (idaku) wa inakatta* "she didn't have such strong misgivings (lit., 'hold misgivings to that extent')" • *donna ren'ai datte* "all love (lit., 'even love of any kind')" • *izure wa sameru mono da* "sooner or later cools" • *katsute wa atsu-atsu datta aite to* "with someone one had been passionately in love with in days gone by" • *samehate-ta (sameru+ hateru) kankei o en'en to jizoku suru koto no hō ga* "the possibility (lit., 'alternative') of continuing forever a cooled relationship" • *samuzamushiku taegatai yō ni omowareta (omou)* "she felt it would be bleak (lit., 'chilly') and hard to bear" • *daigaku-seikatsu o tōshite no bōifurendo wa* "the boyfriend throughout her college life" • *saisho kara asobi no tsumori datta no de* "since he was just for fun from the start (lit., 'she had intended him to be for fun from the start')" • *taishite namikaze mo tatazu (tatsu—tatanaide) ni wakareru koto ga deki-ta* "she was able to separate from him without much of a fuss (lit., 'with-

❖ *gakureki to shūnyū no takasa*: the three things said to be sought in a marriage partner by young Japanese women (i.e., academic background, income, height) are popularly referred to as the *sankō* ("three highs"). ❖ *senchi ijō to*: *to* here is an abbreviation of *to iu yō ni*. ❖ *donna ren'ai datte*: here *datte* (= *de mo*) indicates that a special case is being chosen from a number of similar cases to make a point: cf. the proverb *saru datte ki kara ochiru* (Even monkeys fall from trees). ❖ *sameru mono da*: *mono* here indicates that the preceding statement is a universal tendency. ❖ *katsute wa atsu-atsu*: *atsu-atsu* (colloquial for "piping hot") = passionately in love. ❖ *samehateta kankei*: *hateru* is added to verb stems to indicate that an extreme has been reached: e.g., *tsukarehateta* = dead tired. ❖ *jizoku suru koto no hō ga*: *hō* is used to indicate one of two or more alternatives. ❖ *taegatai*: stem + *gatai* = difficult to ~ . ❖ *asobi*: often used in a broad sense to indicate something one is not serious about. ❖ *namikaze*: lit., "waves and wind"; used idiomatically to refer to discord or quarreling. ❖ *omoshiro-okashii*: = to put aside anything serious or troublesome and concentrate on having a good time; depending on context, might be translated as "to have a barrel of fun." ❖ *shusse-kōsu kara wa hazureta*: *shusse* is getting ahead in the world (more narrowly, getting a promotion at work) and so *shusse-kōsu* is the career track; *hazureru* = (of nails, buttons, etc.) get loose, come off; (of joints) be dislocated; (of targets) miss the mark, be off; (of routes, locations) stray off, be at a distance from. ❖ *risō o e ni egaita yō na*: *e ni egaita yō na* is an idiomatic usage for someone or something that suits something to a tee, that is "the very picture of ~ ."

out wind and waves arising')" • *kare wa omoshiro-okashiku asobu ni wa yokatta ga* "he was fine for joking around and having a good time, but" • *shōrai-teki na shusse-kōsu kara wa hazureta (hazureru) wakamono datta* "he was a young man who had deviated from the course for future success" • *omiai no aite wa* "the man she met through an arranged meeting" • *risō o e ni egaita (egaku) yō na dansei datta* "was like the embodiment of all her dreams (lit., 'like a picture drawn of her ideals')"

だった。由美ちゃんは、そのように結婚したのだった。

一緒に暮らすようになってほどなくわかったのだが、夫はほとんど無趣味だった。本など一冊も読まない。あえていえば仕事が趣味だった。たまに家にいると、パジャマのままゴロゴロしてテレビばかり観ている。

趣味がないから、話題にも乏しい。二人の間に最低必要限度の会話しか成立しない。由美ちゃんは昔のボーイフレンドの機知とユーモアに富んだお喋りをよく思い出すようになった。

そのうち、図体ばかり大きくて、ゴロゴロしている夫が、やけに目ざわりに思えて来た。家の中にばかりいるからいけないのだと想い、「働いてみよう

• *Yumi-chan wa sono yō ni kekkon shita no datta* "that was the way in which Yumi got married" • *issho ni kurasu yō ni natte hodo-naku wakatta (wakaru) no da ga* "she realized it soon after they started living together, but" • *otto wa hotondo mushumi datta* "her husband had almost no personal interests (lit., 'hobbies, pastimes')" • *hon nado issatsu mo yomanai (yomu)* "he didn't read even a single book" • *aete ieba (iu)* "if pressed, you might say" • *shigoto ga shumi datta* "his job was his hobby" • *tama ni ie ni iru to* "on rare occasions when he was at home" • *pajama no mama* "(while) still in his pajamas" • *gorogoro shite terebi bakari mite (miru) iru* "he just lay around watching TV" • *shumi ga nai kara* "since he had no interests" • *wadai ni mo toboshii* "he didn't have much to talk about (lit., 'he was poor in topics of conversation')" • *futari no aida ni* "between the two of them" • *saitei hitsuyō gendo no kaiwa shika seiritsu shinai* "there existed (lit., 'came into being') only the bare minimum level of conversation" • *Yumi-chan wa ~ o yoku omoidasu yō ni natta* "Yumi would frequently recall ~ " • *mukashi no bōifurendo no kichi to yūmoa ni tonda [tomu] oshaberi o* "the conversation of her old boyfriend, which was full of wit and humor" • *sono uchi* "before long" • *zūtai bakari ōkikute* "big in body only" • *gorogoro shite iru otto ga* "her loafing husband" • *yake ni mezawari ni omoete (omou) kita (kuru)* "came

❖ *gorogoro*: onomatopoeic for rumbling sounds like thunder and figurative for idle loafing. ❖ *yūmoa ni tonda*: *ni tomu* = to be rich in, have a wealth of, be full of. ❖ *oshaberi*: used for everyday talking or chatting. ❖ *mezawari ni omoete kita*: *omoeru* indicates that a thought comes naturally to mind without any particular intention. ❖ *"hataraite miyō kashira" to itte mita*: the first *miru* (*miyō*) has the meaning "to try" ("maybe I should try working"); the second *miru* (*mita*) = "to do it and see what happens." *Kashira* is feminine usage equivalent to (but softer than) masculine/feminine *ka*.

to regard him as an awful eyesore" • *ie no naka ni bakari iru kara ikenai no da to omoi (omou)* "thinking that it wasn't working out because she was at home all the time" • *"hataraite (hataraku) miyō (miru) kashira" to itte (iu) mita* "she said, to test the waters, 'Maybe I should find a job'" • *otto wa* "her husband" • *sokuza ni* "on the spot; at once"

かしら」と言ってみた。夫は即座に「その必要はな
い」と答えた。妻を外へ働きに出さずに済むだけの
給料は、稼いでいるはずだから、と言うのだった。
退屈な日々がウツウツとして流れてた。子供でも
生もうかしらと、ふとそう思った。
由美ちゃんは妊娠し、無事子供を生んだ。背の高
いハンサムな夫は出世コースの仕事にかまけて、育
児には全く関知しなかった。彼女はとり残されたよ
うな気がした。小ぎれいではあるがだんらんのない
家庭という檻の中に、つながれているという思いが
つのった。退屈しのぎに生んだ子供は今や、足かせ
となって、二重に彼女を檻の中に縛りつけるのだっ
た。
そんなある日、彼女は風の便りに昔のボーイフレ

• *"Sono hitsuyō wa nai" to kotaeta (kotaeru)* "he replied, 'There's no need for that'" • *tsuma o soto e hataraki ni dasazu (=dasanaide) ni sumu dake no kyūryō wa* "a salary that did not require him to send his wife out to work (lit., 'a salary that would at least allow him not to send his wife out to work')." • *kaseide (kasegu) iru hazu da kara to iu no datta* "he said he thought (lit., 'expected') he was earning ~." • *taikutsu na hibi ga utsu-utsu to shite nagarete (nagareru) 'ta* "boring days passed by cheerless-ly" • *kodomo de mo umō kashira to futo sō omotta (omou)* "it occurred to her, maybe I should have a baby" • *Yumi-chan wa ninshin shi (suru)* "Yumi got pregnant" • *buji kodomo o unda (umu)* "she safely gave birth to a child" • *se no takai hansamu na otto wa* "her tall, handsome hus-band" • *shusse-kōsu no shigoto ni kamakete (kamakeru)* "he was preoc-cupied by his fast-track job" • *ikuji ni wa mattaku kanchi shinakatta* "he concerned himself in no way whatsoever with childrearing" • *kanojo wa torinokosareta (torinokosu) yō na ki ga shita* "she felt she had been left behind (by the world)" • *kogirei de wa aru ga* "it (their home) was neat and tidy, but" • *danran no nai katei to iu ori no naka ni* "in this cage-like household (lit., 'in this cage of a household') with no family warmth" • *tsunagarete (tsunagu) iru to iu omoi ga tsunotta (tsunoru)* "the feeling that she was trapped (lit., 'bound') in ~ grew stronger and stronger" •

❖ *dasazu ni sumu*: the formula *-zu ni sumu* or *-nai de sumu* means that something can be done (brought to a conclusion or settled) without the action indicated by the preceding (negative) verb. ❖ *to iu no datta*: *no* here can be replaced by *koto*, with the meaning "the story was that ~ ." ❖ *shigoto ni kamakete*: = to be absorbed in, engrossed by; has strong negative connotations. ❖ *danran*: original meaning, circle; = for people to gather around and talk in a warm and friendly manner. ❖ *taikutsu-shinogi ni*: set phrase = to pass the time away; as a diversion (*taikutsu* = boredom; *shinogi* (*shinogu*) = endure, stave off). ❖ *kaze no tayori ni*: idiomatic for something heard as a rumor, something told to one by a little bird.

---

taikutsu-shinogi ni unda (*umu*) *kodomo wa* "the child to whom she had given birth just to pass the time" • *imaya ashikase to natte* "had now become a millstone around her neck (lit., 'leg shackles')" • *nijū ni kanojo o ori no naka ni shibaritsukeru no datta* "had doubly bound her inside the cage" • *sonna aru hi* "on one such day" • *kanojo wa kaze no tayori ni* "she heard through the grapevine (lit., 'from tidings on the wind')"

ンドが結婚して今は海外で暮らしているという話を
耳にした。彼の父親が亡くなり、相続した地方都市
の土地と家を売り、オーストラリアに移住したのだ
という。そこで牧場を買い、つつましく人生の新し
いスタートを切ったということだった。
　由美ちゃんは、広々とした牧草と、青い空とを思
い描いた。そこで手に手をとって動物の世話をする
若夫婦の姿を想像した。自分をその妻におきかえて
みたりもした。自然と動物に囲まれて伸び伸びと育
つ子供たちが、眼に見えるようだった。無限の可能
性を秘めた子供たち、若夫婦。彼女は自分が失って
しまったものの大きさに呆然とした。
　だけどね、由美ちゃん。私はやっぱり今のあなた
の生活が、あなたに一番ふさわしいのだと思う。

• *mukashi no bōifurendo ga kekkon shite* "her old boyfriend had married" • *ima wa kaigai de kurashite (kurasu) iru* "he was now living abroad" • *to iu hanashi o mimi ni shita* "she got wind of talk to the effect that ~" • *kare no chichioya ga nakunari (nakunaru)* "his father had passed away" • *sōzoku shita chihō-toshi no tochi to ie o uri (uru)* "he sold the land and house he had inherited in a provincial city" • *Ōsutoraria ni ijū shita no da to iu* "(they) said he had emigrated to Australia" • *soko de bokujō o kai (kau)* "he bought a cattle ranch there" • *tsutsumashiku jinsei no atarashii sutāto o kitta (kiru) to iu koto datta* "he had, on a modest scale, made a new start in life" • *Yumi-chan wa hiro-biro to shita bokusō to aoi sora to o omoiegaita (omoiegaku)* "Yumi pictured (lit., 'drew a picture in thought') spacious grasslands and a blue sky" • *soko de ~ o sōzō shita* "she imagined there ~ " • *te ni te o totte* "hand in hand" • *dōbutsu no sewa o suru wakafūfu no sugata o* "the newlyweds caring for animals" • *jibun o sono tsuma ni okikaete (okikaeru) mitari (miru) mo shita* "she also substituted herself for the wife in her mind" • *shizen to dōbutsu ni kakomarete (kakomu)* "surrounded by animals and nature" • *nobinobi to sodatsu kodomo-tachi ga me ni mieru yō datta* "it was as if she could see in front of her the children growing up free of cares" • *mugen no kanō-sei o himeta (himeru) kodomo-tachi*

❖ *mimi ni shita*: *mimi ni suru* = to hear unintentionally, by chance. ❖ *sutāto o kiru*: can be thought of here as "cutting out" a new start; *kiru* in this sense refers to the commencing of some action: e.g., *totsuzen kuchi o kitta* ("he suddenly spoke up"). ❖ *wakafūfu no sugata*: *sugata* refers to a figure or form; often lost in translation. *Wakafūfu* includes the positive image of happy young newlyweds, not simply a newly married couple. ❖ *okikaete mitari mo shita*: the use of ~*tari* indicates this was one of several things she did. ❖ *da kedo ne*: roughly, "but, you see." Note the change in tone of voice here, with the author addressing Yumi directly, dropping the more friendly "Yumi-chan" (save for one instance) for the more objective and stricter *anata*. ❖ *yappari*: colloquial form of *yahari*; suggests that something is in accordance with one's expectations (possible English translation, "sure enough.")

"children of unlimited potential" • *wakafūfu* "the young newlyweds" • *kanojo wa* "she" • *jibun ga ushinatte (ushinau) shimatta mono no ōkisa ni bōzen to shita* "she was dumfounded at the dimensions of what she had lost" • *da kedo ne* "but listen" • *yappari (yahari)* "after all" • *ima no anata no seikatsu ga anata ni ichiban fusawashii no da to omou* "I think your present life is the one best for (lit., 'most suited to') you"

もし、昔のボーイフレンドと結婚したとしても、あなたは、彼のオーストラリア移住計画に対して、顔色を変えて反対していたと思うのよ。そんな、海のものとも山のものともつかない無謀な人生計画なんて、とんでもないわ、と。

あなたは、安定した生活の保障だけを求めていた、そしてそれを手に入れた。安定ということが退屈と同義語だということは、知らなかったみたいだけど。

• *moshi mukashi no bōifurendo to kekkon shita toshite mo* "even if you had married your old boyfriend" • *kare no Ōsutoraria ijū-keikaku ni taishite* "toward his plan of emigrating to Australia" • *anata wa ~ kaoiro o kaete (kaeru) hantai shite ita to omou no yo* "I definitely think you would have angrily (lit., 'with a change in face color') opposed it" • *sonna* "such a (life plan)" • *umi no mono to mo yama no mono to mo tsukanai (tsuku)* "irrational" • *mubō na jinsei keikaku nante* "such a rash life plan" • *tonde mo nai wa to* "it was utterly ridiculous, (you'd) say" • *anata wa antei shita seikatsu no hoshō dake o motomete (motomeru) ita* "the only thing you wanted (lit., 'sought') was the guarantee of a stable livelihood" • *soshite sore o te ni ireta (ireru)* "and you gained that (lit., 'put it in hand')" • *antei to iu koto ga taikutsu to dōgi-go da to iu koto wa shiranakatta mitai da kedo* "but it seems you didn't know that stability is a synonym for boredom"

❖ *kekkon shita toshite mo*: *-ta* + *toshite* [*mo*] = even if ~ ; somewhat stronger than, e.g., *kekkon shite mo*. ❖ *kaoiro o kaete*: i.e., to become livid with anger. ❖ *umi no mono to mo yama no mono to mo tsukanai*: an idiomatic phrase indicating something unclear or unresolved (lit., "to be neither something from the ocean nor something from the mountains")—to be neither fish nor fowl, to be up in the air; *tsukanai* (from *tsuku* = to stick), meaning not to come to a conclusion or reach a solution. ❖ *nante*: equivalent to *nado to* (and such things as); used belittlingly. ❖ *tonde mo nai wa, to*: *tonde mo nai* is an idiomatic phrase indicating that something is ridiculous or out of the question; *wa*: a sentence-ending particle employed primarily by women in this usage; the sentence or phrase preceding *to* is an example of inversion (or reversal in order), and would logically follow *ni taishite* in the previous sentence.

Sakamoto Ryūichi

The world-renowned musician Sakamoto Ryūichi was born in Tokyo in 1952. After graduating from the Tokyo University of Fine Arts and Music, he released his first solo album and joined with two other musicians to form the techno-pop group Yellow Magic Orchestra (YMO) in 1978. YMO was dissolved five years later and Sakamoto returned to solo work. In addition to composing film music, he has appeared as an actor in *Merry Christmas, Mr. Lawrence* and *The Last Emperor*.

In 1988 he received an Academy Award, along with David Byrne and Cong Su, for the music for *The Last Emperor*. He presently resides in New York City.

His reflections here on the nature of tempo, or "beat," in music and in human life were written in a two-year exchange of letters (1990–92) with the novelist Murakami Ryū published in the magazine *Gekkan kadokawa*. In its somewhat casual and loosely constructed style, it is typical of much writing published in Japan. The version here, slightly abridged, carries the title of the book in which it appears.

First published in *Gekkan kadokawa*. Copyright 1991 by Sakamoto Ryūichi. It also appears in book form in *Tomo yo, mata aō* by Sakamoto Ryūichi and Murakami Ryū. Reprinted by permission of Kadokawa Shoten and the author.

友よ、また逢おう

坂本龍一

今回のレコードは、ビートのあるものとメロディー優先のものと、はっきり分かれてます。ビートのものはなるべく気持ち良く、メロディーものはとてもメランコリックあるいはロマンティックに……という風に。そうしないと、龍もよく知っているぼくのビート拒否症が頭をもたげて、体全体を侵してしまいそうになるからね。

『ビューティ』ではなるべく強制的なビートを避けて、全体的にオーガニック（有機的、反機械的）なリズムで満たされるようにこころがけたんだけど、当然のこととして、乱暴で機械的で強圧的なビート

• *konkai no rekōdo wa* "(my) record this time" • *bīto no aru mono* "ones (tracks) with a (strong) beat" • *merodī yūsen no mono* "ones (tracks) giving priority to melody" • *~to ~ to hakkiri wakarete 'masu [wakarete imasu]* "is clearly divided into ~ and ~ " • *bīto no mono wa* "ones stressing beat" • *narubeku kimochi yoku* "with a distinct, easy-to-follow beat (lit., 'with as much good feeling as possible')" • *merodī-mono wa* "ones stressing melody" • *totemo* "very" • *merankorikku* "melancholic" • *arui-wa* "or" • *romantikku* "romantic" • *ni = ni suru* "to make" • *to iu fū ni* "so that they're (divided in that way)" • *sō shinai to* "otherwise" • *Ryū mo yoku shitte iru boku no bīto kyohi-shō ga* "my 'beat phobia' which you, Ryū, know so well" • *atama o motagete [motageru]* "(my phobia) will rear its head (will assert itself)" • *karada zentai* "all of my body (all of me)" • *okashite [okasu] shimaisō ni naru kara ne* "will threaten to invade, you see" • *"Byūti" de wa* "in *Beauty* (his previous record)" • *narubeku kyōsei-teki na bīto o sakete* "avoiding as much as possible a coercive (compulsive) beat" • *zentai-teki ni* "overall" • *ōganikku* "organic" • *(yūki-teki, han-kikai-teki)* "(organic, non-mechanical [lit., 'anti-mechanical'])" • *rizumu de mitasareru [mitasu] yō ni* "that it would be filled with rhythm" • *kokoro-gaketa n' da kedo* "although I endeavored to (see that ~)" • *tōzen no koto toshite* "naturally enough (of course)" •

❖ *tomo yo*: *tomo*, related to, but independent from, *tomodachi* in usage, likewise means friend or acquaintance: *Masaka no toki no tomo ga shin no tomo* "A friend in need is a friend indeed." *Yo* is a means of calling out to someone. ❖ *konkai no*: note that, according to context, this can refer to either something that has just happened or something that will soon happen. ❖ *wakarete 'masu*: *-te iru* and *-te imasu* are often contracted in speech to *-te 'ru* and *-te 'masu*. ❖ *boku*: a male pronoun for "I," most often used among younger men. ❖ *okashite shimaisō ni naru*: verb stem + *sō* = "to seem, be likely to, threaten to." ❖ *naru kara ne*: by way of explanation, it is not uncommon for Japanese sentences to refer back to the previous sentence explicitly by ending in *kara* or *no de* ("the reason for that is …"). ❖ *Beauty*: the record Sakamoto had released a year or so before the time of writing.

---

ranbō de [de aru] "violent (harsh, jarring)" • *kikai-teki de [de aru]* "mechanical (machine-like)" • *kyōatsu-teki na* "overwhelming (overpowering)"

に支配されている今の世界中のポップスの狭間にあっては、少し頼りなく響いたかもしれない。

いまさらそんなことを、ってあきれられるかもしれないけど、ビートを気持ち良く感じるというのは無反省な状態ということだからね。だいたいビートというのは規則的だろ、だからそれによって集合的な複数の人間が共通の動作をできる。これは誰にとっても外部なビートというものに全員が従順に従わなければ成立しない。すぐれてファシスティックだろ——ぼくはこれを思想的な興味で言ってるんじゃない。ぼくの体がどうしても反応してしまうことを、分析的に言おうとしているだけだ。

ここでぼくの頭にうかぶのはふたつのこと。ひとつは、こないだM・C・ハマーが日本に行った。新

• *bīto ni shihai sarete iru ima no sekai-jū no poppusu* "the pop music which is now dominated throughout the world by a beat (that is violent etc.)" • *hazama ni atte* "in the midst of (lit., 'in between')" • *sukoshi tayori naku hibiita [hibiku] ka mo shirenai* "it may have sounded a little weak" • *ima sara sonna koto o* "(why fret about) such a thing *now* (i.e., at this late date)" • *tte = to* • *akirerareru ka mo shirenai kedo* "you may be amazed (may be taken aback), but" • *bīto o kimochi yoku kanjiru to iu no wa* "to feel the beat pleasingly" • *mu-hansei na jōtai to iu koto da* "(that) is a state of non-awareness (lit., 'non-self-reflection')" • *daitai* "mainly" • *bīto to iu no wa kisoku-teki daro* "beat is regular (methodical), right?" • *da kara* "so" • *sore ni yotte* "by means of it (the beat)" • *shūgō-teki na fukusū no ningen ga* "a number of individuals assembled together" • *kyōtsū no dōsa o dekiru* "can make the same physical movement (can move in unison)" • *kore wa ~ seiritsu shinai* "this (mass movement in unison) ~ will not be realized" • *dare ni totte mo* "for anyone" • *gaibu na bīto to iu mono ni zen'in ga jūjun ni shitagawanakereba [shitagau]* "unless everyone submissively obeys the exterior beat" • *sugurete [sugureru] fashisutikku daro* "it is a fine (example) of fascism" • *kore o shisō-teki na kyōmi de itte 'ru n' ja nai* "I am not saying this from an ideological concern (lit., 'interest')" • *boku no karada ga dōshite mo*

❖ *tayori naku*: lit., "cannot be relied upon"; here used broadly in the sense of "insubstantial" or "feeble." ❖ *ima sara*: lit., "now again." Implies the futility of bringing up a topic that has already been settled or that nothing can be done about now. ❖ *tte akirareru*: *tte* is often used in speech for *to itte*, *to omotte*, *to iu fū ni*, etc., depending on the context. ❖ *kisoku-teki daro*: *daro* is contracted form of *darō*; as used here it calls for the agreement of the reader (said with a rising intonation in speech). ❖ *shūgō-teki na fukusū no ningen*: two ideas are conveyed here: the fact that people have come together as a group but also that they remain individuals. ❖ *sugurete*: lit., "excellent, outstanding." Here used in a sense similar to "blatant"; a literary usage. ❖ *iō to shite iru*: *-ō/-yō + suru* = "try to, intend to." ❖ *konaida*: a contracted form of *kono aida*.

---

hannō shite shimau koto o "the fact that my body couldn't help responding (to the beat)" • *bunseki-teki ni iō to shite iru dake da* "I am simply trying to speak analytically (about the fact that ~)" • *koko de* "in this connection" • *boku no atama ni ukabu no wa* "what comes to mind (lit., 'what floats into my head')" • *futatsu no koto* "two things" • *hitotsu wa* "one of them" • *konaida*: = *kono aida* "recently (the other day)" • *Emu Shī Hamā* "(the musician) M. C. Hammer" • *Nihon ni itta [iku]* "went to Japan"

聞かなんかの記事に、「会場全体がビートの渦で興奮に包まれた」っていうようなことが書かれてあったけど、ぼくには何だかとっても奇妙な光景に見えた。観客達は文字通り「踊らされた」わけだ、言語的コミュニケーションなしに。

もうひとつは、胎児は母体の中にいる間中とぎれなくさまざまなビートを聞き続けている、ということ。これもおそろしく強制的で胎児に他の選択はない。もちろん、これらのビートが胎児にとって生命の絆であり、自己の安全の保証だとしても。

安易にこれらふたつのことを結びつけるのはやめるとしても、こういう想像がすぐぼくの頭に去来する。つまり世界が危険でおそろしく見えるとき、ぼくらは永遠に途切れることない安定した（ある意味

• *shinbun ka nanka no kiji ni* "in an article in the newspaper or someplace" • *"kaijō zentai ga bīto no uzu de kōfun ni tsutsumareta [tsutsumu]"* "'the whole concert hall was in a frenzy (lit., "enveloped in a whirlpool of excitement") from the whirlpool of a beat'" • *tte iu yō na koto ga kakarete atta kedo* "something like that was written, but" • *boku ni wa* "to me" • *nan da ka* "somehow" • *tottemo [totemo] kimyō na kōkei ni mieta* "it was (lit., 'looked like') a very strange sight" • *kankyakutachi wa* "the spectators (audience)" • *moji-dōri "odorasareta" wake da* "were literally 'dancing' (being made to dance)" • *gengo-teki komyunikēshon nashi ni* "without verbal communication (i.e., without the benefit of language)" • *mō hitotsu wa, ~ , to iu koto* "the other (of the two things) was" • *taiji wa botai no naka ni iru aida-jū* "the fetus, all the while it is in its mother's body" • *togirenaku samazama na bīto o kikitsuzukete iru* "continues to hear various beats without a break" • *osoroshiku [osoroshii] kyōsei-teki de [de aru]* "is dreadfully compulsory" • *taiji ni hoka no sentaku wa nai* "the fetus has no other choice (no choice in the matter)" • *mochiron, ~ da toshite mo* "even, of course, though" • *korera no bīto ga taiji ni totte seimei no kizuna de ari [de aru]* "these beats are lifelines (lit., 'ties, bonds') for the fetus" • *jiko no anzen no hoshō da* "are the guarantee of its own safety" • *an'i ni* "easily (facile-

❖ *nan da ka*: a common phrase meaning "somehow" or "somehow or other." ❖ *tottemo (totemo)*: the doubling of the *t* intensifies the meaning. ❖ *moji-dōri "odorasareta"*: the common figurative meaning of *odorasareta* is "to be controlled like a puppet"; here *moji-dōri* ("literally") indicates that both figurative and literal meanings ("to be made to dance") are intended. ❖ *kankyaku-tachi wa ~ wake da, gengō-teki ~ nashi ni*: the reversal of clauses for emphasis is common in Japanese. ❖ *kiki-tsuzukete iru*: stem + *tsuzukeru* = continue ~ ing. ❖ *tsumari*: often used to start an explanation or elaboration of a previous statement. ❖ *togireru koto nai*: note that *togireru* is written in *kanji* here and in *hiragana* in the first sentence of the previous paragraph; the decision often seems to be a subjective one based on balance within a section or a practical one for adjusting the length of a printed line.

---

ly)" • *korera futatsu no koto o musubitsukeru no wa* "what links these two things together" • *yameru to shite mo* "even if we give up (the idea of linking them)" • *kō iu sōzō ga* "this sort of notion" • *sugu* "soon" • *boku no atama ni* "in my head (my mind)" • *kyorai suru* "recurs (lit., 'comes and goes')" • *tsumari* "that is (in other words)" • *sekai ga kiken de osoroshiku mieru toki* "when the world appears dangerous and frightening" • *bokura wa eien ni togireru koto nai antei shita ~ bīto ni hitatte [hitaru] itai* "we want to be bathed in a never-ending, stable (secure) ~ beat"

で、機械的な）ビートに浸っていたい、という意識下の欲求が強くあらわれるのではないか……。そして多分この欲求じたいは自然なもので、むしろ防御的なものかもしれない。特にニューヨークで見かけるハウス・ミュージックをやってる若い黒人達がみんなすごく優しくて、ひたすら気持ちの良いグルーヴだけを求めて何時間もヘッドフォーンをしてるのを見ると、これは胎内回帰だと思う。

ぼく自身も湾岸戦争が終わったあと、戦争じたいへの心配よりも終わったあとの人々の傲慢さにひどく傷ついて――まあ、人間に明るい未来があるなんて最初から思っていないけど――それがぼくにレコーディングに集中させることになった気がする。

えーと、ちょっと論旨が乱れてる気もするけど、

• *(aru imi de kikai-teki na)* "(in a certain sense a mechanical [beat])" • *to iu ishiki-ka no yokkyū ga tsuyoku arawareru no de wa nai ka* "doesn't such a subconscious craving strongly appear?" • *soshite* "and" • *tabun kono yokkyū jitai wa shizen na mono de [de aru]* "this craving itself is probably a natural thing" • *mushiro bōgyo-teki na mono ka mo shirenai* "it might even be something defensive (lit., 'defensive rather than [a craving]')" • *toku ni* "especially" • *Nyūyōku de mikakeru hausu myūjikku o yatte 'ru [yatte iru] wakai kokujin-tachi ga* "young blacks who you come across in New York playing house music (in clubs)" • *minna sugoku yasashikute* "all of them are very mild (lit., 'gentle')" • *hitasura kimochi no yoi gurūbu dake o motomete [motomeru]* "searching single-mindedly (simply devoted only to searching) for a groove with a good feeling" • *nan-jikan mo heddofōn o shite 'ru [shite iru] no o miru to* "when I see them spending hours with their headphones on" • *kore wa tainai-kaiki da to omou* "I think that this is a return to the womb" • *boku jishin mo* "I myself also" • *Wangan-sensō ga owatta ato* "after the Gulf War ended" • *sensō jitai e no shinpai yori mo* "rather than worrying about the war itself" • *owatta ato no hitobito no gōman-sa ni hidoku kizu-tsuite [kizu-tsuku]* "I was terribly wounded by people's arrogance after it ended" • *mā* "oh, well" • *ningen ni akarui mirai ga aru nante*

❖ *yatte 'ru*: = *yatte iru.* ❖ *shite 'ru*: = *shite iru.* ❖ *Wangan-sensō*: the Gulf War of early 1991 (Sakamoto's letter is dated April 1991). ❖ *kizu-tsuite*: lit., "hurt physically or damaged"; the common figurative meaning is emotionally hurt or wounded. ❖ *mā*: in this sense indicates a restraining of one's own or someone else's emotion; said here with some resignation and irony. Very common in speech. ❖ *ēto*: uuh, uumn; a common hesitation sound in speech while searching for the next word or thing to talk about.

---

saisho kara omotte inai kedo "I never thought that humankind had much of a bright future in the first place, but" • *sore ga boku ni rekōdingu ni shūchū saseru koto ni natta ki ga suru* "I have a feeling that that's what caused me to concentrate on my recording" • *ēto* "well" • *chotto ronshi ga midarete 'ru [midarete iru] ki mo suru* "I have the feeling that my argument may have become a bit confused (lit., 'snarled')"

ビートにはふた通りあるのかな？　攻撃的で人を抑圧するビートと、優しくて人を保護するビートと……？　どちらもぼくには人間の弱さを思わせる。外界や外部に対して奴隷のように従うか、母体にもぐりこんでひたすら保護を求めるか……。

というわけで今回のぼくのレコードは、おろかで弱い人間（もちろん自分も含む）に対する愛とあきらめのビートで満ちることになるでしょう。

龍とミホさんと『トパーズ』のみなさん、ご自愛ください。

坂本龍一

• *bīto ni wa futa-tōri aru no ka na?* "aren't there two types of beat?" • *kōgeki-teki de [de aru] hito o yokuatsu suru bīto to* "a beat that is aggressive and oppresses people and" • *yasashikute hito o hogo suru bīto to* "and a beat that is gentle and protects people" • *dochira mo* "both of them" • *boku ni wa ningen no yowasa o omowaseru* "make me think of the frailty (lit., 'weakness') of human beings" • *gaikai ya gaibu ni taishite* "toward the outside or external world" • *dorei no yō ni shitagau ka* "submit slavishly" • *botai ni mogurikonde [mogurikomu] hitasura hogo o motomeru ka* "or crawl into the womb (lit., 'mother's body') and single-mindedly seek protection" • *to iu wake de* "and so" • *konkai no boku no rekōdo wa* "my record this time" • *oroka de [de aru] yowai ningen ~ ni taisuru* "for foolish and frail humanity ~ " • *(mochiron jibun mo fukumu)* "of course, myself included" • *ai to akirame no bīto de michiru koto ni naru deshō* "it will most likely be full of the beat of love and resignation" • *Ryū to Miho-san to "Topāzu" no mina-san* "Ryū and Miho and everyone at 'Topaz'" • *gojiai kudasai* "take care of yourself (lit., 'please love yourselves')"

❖ *gaikai, gaibu*: virtual synonyms ❖ *shitagau ka ~ motomeru ka*: ~ *ka* ~ *ka* = either ~ or ~ (i.e., an elaboration of mankind's weakness in the previous sentence). ❖ *mogurikonde*: -*komu* is often added to the stem of a verb to emphasize the action of moving inward or insertion (*oshikomu, sashikomu,* etc.). ❖ *to iu wake de*: commonly used in concluding a given topic or talk. ❖ *Topāzu*: at the time, Murakami Ryū was directing a movie called *Topaz*, starring the actress Nikaidō Miho. ❖ *gojiai kudasai*: a common but formal expression found in correspondence.

Tawara Machi

Born in Osaka in 1962 and a graduate of Waseda University, Tawara Machi worked as a high school teacher of Japanese language and literature for four years prior to the spectacular success of her first book of poetry in 1987. *Sarada kinenbi* (published in two English translations as *Salad Anniversary*), a collection of short poems in the traditional five-line *tanka* format dealing in colloquial language with love and other everyday problems of young Japanese women, won the hearts of a younger generation of readers and sold some three million copies. She has published several volumes of essays and interviews, introductions to the classics for modern readers, and another volume of poetry, *Mō hitotsu no ai*; she is also a frequent guest on television programs, particularly those dealing with art and literature.

Her essay here, relating an experience from her teaching days, reflects the light but elegant style of her writing.

First published in *Monbu jihō*. Copyright 1989 by Tawara Machi. The essay also appears in the author's book *Ringo no namida*. Reprinted by permission of Bungei Shunju and the author.

心に届く言葉

俵　万智

　教職を退いて、半年がたった。生徒たちのことが、折にふれて思い出される。その中には、いわゆる「ワル」だったヤツの顔が少なくない。

　久しぶりに実家に帰って弟の部屋を覗くと、奇怪なロックバンドのCDが置いてある。弟は高校二年生。ちょうど私の教えていた生徒たちと同じ年頃だ。そういえばこのロックバンド、生徒たちにも人気があったっけ……。ぼんやりと歌詞カードを眺めていた。

　そのとき、ふと思い出されたのがM君の顔である。一年生の頃からのツッパリで、髪を赤く染めていた。

• *kokoro ni todoku kotoba* "words which strike at the heart (lit., 'words that reach the heart')" • *kyōshoku o shirizoite [shirizoku]* "leaving my teaching position" • *hantoshi ga tatta [tatsu]* "half a year has passed" • *seito-tachi no koto* "things about my students" • *ori ni furete* "on occasion; now and then" • *omoidasareru [omoidasu]* "are remembered (by me); come to mind" • *sono naka ni wa* "among them" • *iwayuru "waru" datta yatsu no kao ga* "the faces of those who were so-called bad boys" • *sukunaku nai* "there are not a few" • *hisashiburi ni jikka ni kaette [kaeru]* "I returned home after some time" • *otōto no heya o nozoku to* "when I glanced into my younger brother's room" • *kikai na rokkubando no shī dī ga oite [oku] aru* "a a weird rock band's CD was laying there" • *otōto wa kōkō ni-nensei* "my younger brother (is) a second-year student in high school" • *chōdo ~ to onaji toshigoro* "exactly the same age as ~ " • *watashi no oshiete ita seito-tachi* "the students I was teaching" • *sō ieba* "for that matter, actually" • *kono rokkubando* "this rock band" • *seito-tachi ni mo ninki ga atta kke* "were popular, I remembered, with my students, too" • *bonyari to* "absently; abstractedly" • *kashi-kādo o nagamete ita* "I gazed at the lyric sheet (that came with the CD)" • *sono toki* "it was then" • *futo omoidasareta [omoidasu] no ga* "what I happened to recall" • *Emu-kun no kao de aru* "was the face of student M •

❖ *seito-tachi no koto*: *koto* here, in dictionary definition, refers to circumstances about, and limited to, the modifying word preceding it. ❖ *ori ni furete*: lit., "touching a fold." *Ori* is the noun form of *oru* (fold) and here refers figuratively to a juncture, point in time, or opportunity; the set phrase *ori ni fureru* = "when one has the chance, when opportunity presents itself." ❖ *waru, yatsu*: *waru* is the colloquial noun form of *warui*. *Yatsu* has a number of meanings, most of which are colloquial or verging on slang (e.g., "things/stuff"). Here it is close to "guy, joker." *Katakana* here functions as do quotation marks or italics in English. ❖ *jikka*: lit., "real home"; where one was born or one's parents live. Used under old Japanese civil law to distinguish the home one was born into from the home one married into or was adopted into. ❖ *sō ieba*: lit., "if one says (mentions) that (this comes to mind)." A common transition to indicate something just mentioned reminds one of something else; similar to "that reminds me" or "now that you mention it." ❖ *atta kke*: the informal *kke* is used when recollecting (Oh, that's right. It was popular with my students, too.) ❖ *tsuppari*: from *tsupparu* (a combination of *tsuku* [to thrust] and *haru* [to stretch tight or extend]). While the verb and noun have a number of related meanings, the meaning here (being rebellious or contrary-minded) is generally applied to teenagers. ❖ *somete ita*: using a reddish hair rinse is a common form of rebellion among high school students (Japanese schools enforce strict dress codes).

---

ichi-nensei no koro kara "from the time he was a first-year student" • *tsuppari de [de aru]* "he was rebellious" • *kami o akaku somete ita* "he dyed his hair red"

私の古典の時間など、寝ているか窓の外をぼーっと見ているか。さもなくば、机の下にマンガを広げていた。なんとか彼に振りむいてもらおうと、常に意識して、やさしい質問をしたり、休み時間に話しかけたり、一生懸命だった。私は、自分で言うのもナンだが、かつてはいわゆる優等生。だからM君のようなタイプの生徒が、気になって仕方がない。ただし「気になる」というのは、腹が立つというのとは違う。むしろ、好き嫌いで言えば、私はワルたちが好きだった。

「なんで古典なんか勉強しなきゃなんないんだよォ。こんなもん読めなくたって、生きていけるぜ」

「先生さぁ、金持ちになったんだから、教師なんてさっさとやめちゃえば」

- *watashi no koten no jikan nado* "(during) my classics time (class), say"
- *nete iru ka mado no soto o bōtto mite iru ka* "he was either sleeping or staring out the window" • *samonakuba* "or else (lit., 'if not that')" • *tsukue no shita ni* "(hidden) under his desk" • *manga o hirogete [hirogeru] ita* "he had a comic book open" • *nantoka* "somehow or other" • *kare ni furimuite [furimuku] moraō to* "trying to get his attention (lit., ' ~ to get him to turn [toward me]')" • *tsune ni ishiki shite* "I was always aware of him" • *yasashii shitsumon o shitari* "I would ask him an easy question" • *yasumi-jikan ni hanashikaketari* "I would speak to him during the recess" • *isshō-kenmei datta* "I did my best" • *jibun de iu no mo nan da ga* "if I say so myself" • *katsute wa* "in the past; once upon a time" • *iwayuru yūtō-sei* "I was a so-called prize pupil" • *da kara* "that's why" • *Emu-kun no yō na taipu no seito* "students of M's type" • *ki ni natte shikata ga nai* "really bothered me (lit., 'bothered me and there was nothing I could do about it')" • *tadashi* "and yet" • *"ki ni naru" to iu no wa* "when I say 'really bothered me'" • *hara ga tatsu to iu no to wa chigau* "that's different from being angry" • *mushiro* "rather" • *suki-kirai de ieba* "if I had to say whether I liked or disliked them (as far as my own likes and dislikes are concerned)" • *watashi wa waru-tachi ga suki datta* "I liked the bad boys" • *nande ~ benkyō shinakya nannai n' da yo* "what

❖ *koten no jikan nado*: *nado* indicates that the classics class is mentioned as one possibility, with the meaning of "for example." ❖ *samonakuba*: also *samonakereba*, both slightly literary; either might be paraphrased as *sō de nakereba*, meaning here basically "or else" but in another context possibly "otherwise": e.g., *kanojo wa osoku made zangyō shite iru darō. Samonakereba, ima-doki uchi ni kaette iru hazu da.* "She is probably working late. Otherwise she would be home by now." ❖ *-te moraō to*: *-ō/-yō to suru* = to try to get ~. ❖ *shitari ~ hanashikaketari*: ~ *tari* ~ *tari suru* = to do things like -ing and -ing. ❖ *jibun de iu no mo nan da ga*: lit., "even though I say so myself"; set phrase with a self-deprecatory tone, the *katakana* for *nan* as emphasis. ❖ *katsute*: also pronounced *katte*, *katsute* goes back to readings of Chinese texts in the Heian period; here refers to an occurence in the past with a sense of recall. ❖ *ki ni natte shikata ga nai*: *shikata ga nai* is used idiomatically with the *-te* form of verbs or adjectives to stress one's emotions; the adjective can be repeated (*okashikute okashikute shikata ga nakatta* "It was just so funny; it was so funny I couldn't stand it)." ❖ ~ *to wa chigau*: *A wa B to chigau* = A is different from B. ❖ *suki-kirai de ieba*: *A, B de ieba* = talking about A and B, choosing between A and B. ❖ *nande*: more colloquial and rougher than *naze*. ❖ *benkyō shinakya nannai*: rough contraction of *benkyō shinakereba naranai*. ❖ *yō* (*yo*): emphatic particles are lengthened for emphasis; here, as well as in the contractions, we see the rebelliousness of the student. ❖ *konna mon*: = *konna mono*; contractions characterize rough or uneducated speech. ❖ *yomenakutatte*: standard *yomenakute mo* is reinforced by the emphatic *tatte*. ❖ *ikite ikeru*: idiomatic = "to get by, make ends meet." ❖ *ze*: emphatic particle, used mainly by men. ❖ *sā* (*sa*): emphatic particles can appear after nouns or phrases, similar to "you know" in English, here lengthened for effect. ❖ *kanemochi*: i.e., after the success of Tawara's book *Salad Anniversary*. ❖ *nante*: a contraction of *nado to* (lit., "and such and"); synonymous with *nado* and *nanka*, but like the latter colloquial and often belittling. ❖ *sassa to*: originally the sound of waves, the wind, paper being torn, etc.; secondarily quick actions, often with slightly negative connotations, as here. ❖ *yamechaeba*: contracted form of *yamete shimaeba*; the *-ba* or *-tara* forms are often used for suggestions.

---

do we have to study ~ for" • *koten nanka* "classics and that kind of stuff" • *konna mon* ("this kind of junk") = *konna mono* • *yomenakutatte* "even if you can't read" • *ikite ikeru ze* "you can live OK" • *sensei sā* "hey, Teach (direct address)" • *kanemochi ni natta n' da kara* "since you're rich now" • *kyōshi* "(the profession of) a teacher (i.e., teaching)" • *nante* "and stuff like that" • *sassa to yamechaeba* "why don't you just up and quit"

彼らの率直な言葉には、しばしば絶句させられた
が、きらりと光る批評の目が感じられることもあっ
て、会話は楽しかった。
　期末試験の前日、M君が喫煙で謹慎処分になった
ことがある。そういう場合は「相談室」という部屋
で一人で試験を受けるのが慣例だ。私も古典の試験
監督をしに、相談室へ行った。三十分もたたないう
ちに「あーあ」という顔をして、解答用紙を裏返し
してしまうM君。「もうちょっと考えたら?」とい
う私を無視して、落書きを始めた。
　まあ仕方ないか、と私もあきらめて窓の外を見て
いる。私にとっては宝石箱のような古典の世界も、
彼にとっては苦痛以外の何ものでもない。その素晴
しさを伝えきれない自分にも責任はあるわけだから。

- *karera no* "their" • *sotchoku na kotoba* "plain speaking" • *shibashiba* "often" • *zekku saserareta ga* "was speechless (lit., 'was made speechless'), but" • *kirari to hikaru hihyō no me ga kanjirareru koto mo atte* "I noticed (or felt) a glitter of criticism in their eyes as well, and" • *kaiwa wa tanoshikatta* "it was fun talking (with them) (lit., 'the conversation was fun')" • *kimatsu-shiken no zenjitsu* "the day before final exams (*kimatsu* = 'period end')" • *Emu-kun ga kitsuen de kinshin-shobun ni natta* "M was punished for smoking" • *sō iu bāi wa* "in such cases" • *"sōdan-shitsu" to iu heya de* "in the room called the Consultation Room" • *hitori de shiken o ukeru no ga kanrei da* "it was customary to take exams alone" • *watashi mo ~ sōdan-shitsu e itta [iku]* "I too ~ went to the Consultation Room" • *koten no shiken-kantoku o shi ni [suru no ni]* "in order to act as the supervisor of testing in the classics" • *sanjuppun mo tatanai uchi ni* "before even thirty minutes had passed" • *"āa" to iu kao o shite* "looking fed up" • *kaitō-yōshi o uragaeshi shite shimau Emu-kun* "(there was) M, turning over his answer sheet (to indicate he was finished)" • *"mō chotto kangaetara?" to iu watashi o mushi shite*: "he ignored my saying, 'How about thinking about it a little more'" • *rakugaki o hajimeta* "he started doodling" • *mā shikata nai ka, to* "(thinking) oh well, it can't be helped" • *watashi mo akiramete* "I also gave up" • *mado no*

❖ *kinshin-shobun ni natta*: *kinshin* = a punishment of confinement; *shobun ni naru* = to be the object of a legal action or punishment (compare *shobun ni suru* and *shobun o ukeru*); thus, the meaning is that M was punished by being ordered to confine himself to his home for a certain period of time. ❖ *sōdan-shitsu*: from the verb *sōdan suru* = to talk over a problem; confer ❖ *kanrei*: largely synonymous with *shūkan* (習慣; "custom"), but whereas *shūkan* can be used about personal matters, *kanrei* generally refers to official matters. ❖ *tatanai uchi ni*: *uchi ni* = in the interval …; preceding by a negative verb, it is generally translated as "before something had happened"; preceded by a noun (e.g., *asa no uchi ni*), it is usually translated "during" or "in" (during the morning hours or in the morning). ❖ *"āa" to iu kao o shite*: lit., "making a face that says 'aah,' (I'm fed up)"; i.e., he looked as though he wanted to sigh in disgust; *āa* is the sound (rising on the third *a*) made when sighing with boredom, exasperation, resignation, etc. ❖ *uragaeshi shite*: *uragaeshi (ni) suru* = to turn something upside down. ❖ *mō chotto kangaetara?" to iu watashi o mushi shite*: since *watashi* (modified by the preceding phrase) is the object of the verb *mushi suru*, the whole might be translated literally as follows: "(he) ignored me, who said, "Why don't you think about it a little more?" ❖ *rakugaki*: from *rakusho* (落書; lit., "dropped writings") of the Heian period, when it referred to anonymous, antisocial writings that were dropped here and there for people to pick up and read. ❖ ~ *igai no nanimono de mo nai*: a set phrase; to be nothing other than ~ , to be just ~ . ❖ *tsutaekirenai*: verb stem + *kirenai* = to be unable to do something completely or thoroughly. ❖ *aru wake da kara*: this sentence, ending in *da kara* as it does, gives the reason for the author's feelings and actions in the previous sentence.

---

soto o mite iru "I was looking out the window" • *watashi ni totte wa* "for me" • *hōseki-bako no yō na koten no sekai mo* "even the world of the classics, which is like a treasure chest (lit., 'jewel box')" • *kare ni totte wa* "for him" • *kutsū igai no nanimono de mo nai* "is nothing but a source of pain" • *sono subarashisa* "that wonderfulness" • *tsutaekirenai jibun ni mo* "for myself, who was unable adequately to convey (it)" • *sekinin wa aru wake da kara* "since it is clear that I bear some responsibility for it"

ふとM君のほうへ目をやると、何やらずいぶん熱心に書いている。目で文字を追うと、詩のようなものなので、ちょっとびっくりした。しかも、なかなかいい。きゅうっと胸をしめつけられるような言葉づかいで、青春の抵抗めいたものが綴られている。

「それ、M君の詩?」と思わず聞くと、パッと顔を赤らめて「うん、尾崎豊だよ。先生、知らないの?」と言う。弟からも聞いたことのあるロックシンガーの名前だった。「こういうのだったら、暗記できるのね」と冷やかしながら私は、何かほっとするような嬉しさを感じていた。彼の心を捉えることのできる言葉が、やはりちゃんとあるのだ。ならば私の言葉も、いつかは彼の心に、届くことがあるかもしれない。

• *futo Emu-kun no hō e me o yaru to* "when I happened to look in M's direction" • *nani yara zuibun nesshin ni kaite iru* "he is (was) writing furiously away at something or other" • *me de moji o ou to* "when I ran my eyes over the letters" • *shi no yō na mono na no de* "since it looked like poetry (lit., 'it was something like a poem')" • *chotto bikkuri shita* "I was a bit startled" • *shikamo* "moreover" • *nakanaka ii* "it was quite good" • *kyūtto mune o shimetsukerareru yō na kotoba-zukai de* "in language such as to strike at one's heart" • *seishun no teikō-meita mono ga tsuzurarete iru* "it wrote of the rebelliousness of youth (lit., 'the springtime of life')" • *sore, Emu-kun no shi?* "Is that your poem, M?" • *to omowazu kiku to* "when I asked without thinking" • *patto kao o akaramete* "he suddenly grew red in the face" • *uun*: "unh-unh" • *Ozaki Yutaka da yo* "it's Ozaki Yutaka" • *sensei* "Teacher (direct address)" • *shiranai no?* "you don't know him?" • *to iu* "he says" • *otōto kara mo kiita koto no aru rokkushingā no namae datta* "it was the name of a rock singer I had also heard about from my younger brother" • *kō iu no dattara* "if it's this kind (of verse)" • *anki dekiru no ne* "you can memorize it, can't you" • *to hiyakashinagara [hiyakasu]* "I said while teasing him" • *nanika hotto suru yō na ureshisa o* "a happiness mixed with relief (lit., 'a happiness somehow like relief')" • *kanjite ita* "I felt" • *kare no kokoro o toraeru*

❖ *me o yaru*: to turn (direct) one's eyes. ❖ *nani yara*: a set phrase meaning "something or other" ❖ *kyūtto mune o shimetsukerareru*: lit., "the heart is tightly wrung"; *kyūtto* is used for tightening or squeezing something, as a belt or bottle cap. ❖ *teikō-meita*: ~ + *meita* = ~-like, ~-ish; from the verb *meku*, which can be used in this fashion in both the present and past tenses. ❖ *tsuzurarete iru*: from *tsuzuru*, which has a number of meanings, including spell, write, and patch together. ❖ *patto*: in reference to something that happens suddenly or spreads quickly; here in *katakana* for emphasis. ❖ *Ozaki Yutaka*: a well-known rock singer who died in 1992 at the age of twenty-six. ❖ *shiranai no?*: *no* (with a rising intonation) is often used for emphasis in asking questions, more often by women. ❖ *nanika*: often used to mean "some kind of, a kind of." ❖ *watashi no kotoba mo*: here used in the broader sense of "What I was trying to get across to him (about the classics)."

---

koto no dekiru kotoba ga "words that could capture his heart" • *yahari chanto aru no da* "do exist after all" • *naraba* "if so" • *watashi no kotoba mo* "my words also" • *itsuka wa* "some time" • *kare no kokoro ni, todoku* "will touch (lit., 'reach') his heart" • *koto ga aru ka mo shirenai* "it could be that ~ "

Nejime Shōichi

The poet and author Nejime Shōichi, born in Tokyo in 1948, also runs a folk-craft shop, the Nejime Mingei Ten. He brought a new comic sensibility to Japanese poetry, as well as the controversial use of sexually explicit vocabulary. Known for his public poetry readings and frequent television and radio appearances, he started moving to fiction in the late 1980s. In 1989 he won the prestigious Naoki Prize for *Kōenji junjō shōtengai*, an autobiographically based novel about growing up in Tokyo.

His essay here, on pondering what to do with the money accompanying the Naoki Prize, first appeared in a weekly column in *Shūkan yomiuri*. Written in a lively style, it is full of idiomatic expressions that every foreign student of Japanese should know.

First published in *Shūkan yomiuri*. Copyright 1990 by Nejime Shōichi. The essay also appears in the author's book *Gokinjo paradaisu*. Reprinted by permission of Yomiuri Shinbun and the author.

昼寝をしている私の直木賞百万円

ねじめ正一

東京株式が大暴落だそうである。一時期はナントカ指数だかカントカ株価だかが三万八千円もしていたのに、あっという間に三万五千円を割り三万円を割り、三月の二十二日にはとうとう二万九千円も割ったという。

二月の衆議院選のとき、「我が党が負けると株が下がる」と演説したのはたしか自民党の金丸サンだが（ついでながら、この人の眉毛はいつ見てもおもしろい。タワシというより針金眉毛だ）、選挙が、自民党の勝利に終わったのに、やっぱり株は下がってしまったわけである。

• *hirune o shite iru* "taking a nap" • *watashi no Naoki-shō hyakuman-en* "my ¥1 million Naoki Prize (money)" • *Tōkyō kabushiki* "stock (prices) on the Tokyo Exchange" • *daibōraku da* "have plunged sharply" • *sō de aru* "I hear; it has been reported" • *ichi-jiki wa* "at one time" • *nantoka shisū da ka kantoka kabuka da ka ga* "the so-and-so Index or the such-and-such Quotation" • *san-man hassen-en mo shite ita no ni* "although it stood at ¥38,000" • *atto iu ma ni* "in the wink of an eye" • *sanman gosen-en o wari [waru]* "break the ¥35,000 level; fall below ¥35,000" • *san-man-en o wari [waru]* "fall below ¥30,000" • *sangatsu no nijūni-nichi ni wa* "on March 22" • *tōtō* "finally; in the end" • *niman kyūsen-en mo watta to iu* "(they) say it even fell below ¥29,000" • *nigatsu no shūgi-in–sen[kyō] no toki* "at the time of the February election for the House of Representatives" • *wagatō [seitō] ga makeru to* "if our (political) party loses" • *kabu ga sagaru* "stock (prices) will fall" • *to enzetsu shita no wa* "the one who said (this) in a speech (was)" • *tashika Jimin-tō no Kanemaru-san da ga* "was, if I remember correctly, Mr. Kanemaru of the LDP (Liberal Democratic Party), but" • *tsuidenagara* "by the way; incidentally" • *kono hito no mayuge wa* "this man's (lit., 'this person's') eyebrows" • *itsu mite mo omoshiroi* "are interesting whenever you see them" • *tawashi to iu yori* "rather than a scrubbing brush" • *harigane-*

❖ *hirune o shite iru*: *hirune o suru* = lit., "to take a nap"; most often in reference to human beings but also widely used in a figurative sense; here modifying the ¥1 million. ❖ *Naoki-shō*: prestigious literary prize founded in 1935 in honor of the novelist Naoki Sanjūgo (1891–1934). ❖ *Tōkyō kabushiki*: refers to the slump in the stock markets in New York and Tokyo in 1989 (the essay is dated April 15, 1990). ❖ *nantoka ~ kantoka*: used in place of names one can't remember, are unimportant, thought trival, etc.; the *katakana* adds a humorous touch. ❖ *da ka ~ da ka*: similar to ~ *to ka ~ to ka* in giving alternatives from a larger possible list. ❖ *atto iu ma ni*: lit., "in the time/space of saying ah." ❖ *wagatō*: *waga* can be prefixed to certain nouns and is equivalent to *wareware no*. ❖ *tashika*: the literal meaning is "certainly," but the connotation is "I think it was." *Kanemaru-san*: Kanemaru Shin, an influential power broker in the LDP, to be implicated in a corruption and tax-evasion scandal which broke in 1993. The *katakana*-ization of *san* can be seen as reducing Kanemaru to the level of a cartoon character. ❖ *tsuidenagara*: commonly introduces a parenthetical comment; synonymous with *tsuide ni*. ❖ *yappari*: colloquial form of *yahari*. ❖ *shimatta wake*: *wake* literally means "reason," but here it is a nominalizer, changing a verb into a noun; in this usage, it has the same function as *no* and (*to iu*) *koto*.

---

mayuge da "they are wire-eyebrows" • *senkyō ga, Jimin-tō no shōri ni owatta no ni* "even though the election ended in an LDP victory" • *yappari [yahari] kabu wa sagatte shimatta wake de aru* "sure enough, stock (prices) fell"

ユユしきことだ。
タイヘンなことだ。
とんでもないことだ。

といっても、私が株をやっているわけではない。
それどころか、生まれてこのかた、証券会社とお付き合いしたこともない。
ねじめ民芸店店主というれっきとした商人経験がありながら、いわゆる利殖というものに私はとんと弱い。

百円千円、せいぜい一万円単位なら暗算だってできるし、釣り銭だって間違いなく（たまには間違えるが）渡せるものの、これは足し算引き算の世界で、掛け算割り算、ときによっては微分積分まで必要に

• *yuyushiki koto da* "it's a serious matter" • *taihen na koto da* "it's a terrible thing" • *tonde mo nai koto da* "it's outrageous" • *to itte mo* "having said that; nevertheless (lit., 'even though I say')" • *watashi ga kabu o yatte iru wake de wa nai* "I myself do not dabble in stocks" • *sore dokoro ka* "far from it" • *umarete kono kata* "(never) in my born days" • *shōken-gaisha to otsukiai shita koto mo nai* "I have never had any dealings with a brokerage firm" • *Nejime mingei-ten tenshu* "proprietor of the Nejime Folkcraft Shop" • *to iu rekki to shita shōnin-keiken ga arinagara [aru + nagara]* "while I do have (such an) unimpeachable career (lit., 'experience') as a merchant" • *iwayuru rishoku to iu mono ni watashi wa tonto yowai* "I am no good (lit., 'awfully weak') at real moneymaking" • *hyaku-en sen-en, seizei ichiman-en tan'i nara* "if it is a matter of units of ¥100, ¥1,000, or at most ¥10,000" • *anzan datte dekiru shi* "I can even calculate it in my head, and" • *tsurisen datte machigai naku (~) wataseru [watasu] mono no* "although I can also make (lit., 'hand over') change without mistakes" • *(tama ni wa machigaeru ga)* "(though every so often I do make a mistake)" • *kore wa tashizan hikizan no sekai de [de aru]* "this is the world of addition and subtraction" • *kakezan warizan* "multiplication and division" • *toki ni yotte wa* "depending on the situation (lit., 'according to the time')" • *bibun sekibun made hitsuyō ni narisō na*

❖ *yuyushiki*: = *yuyushii*; *-shiki* is an older ending of Japanese adjectives from classical Japanese, but this particular form is commonly used in modern Japanese; *katakana* here shows that the matter is not as serious as the words would indicate. ❖ *to itte mo*: lit., "even saying ~ "; the meaning is "but" or "however," but as here, a bit of the literal meaning sometimes remains. ❖ *sore dokoro ka*: noun + *dokoro ka* = far from ~. ❖ *umarete kono kata*: lit., "this side of being born"; a common set phrase. ❖ *otsukiai*: usually used for social dealings with people and organizations. ❖ *Nejime Mingei-ten*: the name of Nejime's folk-craft shop. ❖ *arinagara*: verb stem + *nagara* = while -ing. ❖ *yowai*: *yowai* and *tsuyoi* are often used idiomatically for being poor or good at some activity such as mathematics or drinking. ❖ *anzan datte*: *datte* is an intensifier largely synonymous with *de mo* and *de sae mo*. ❖ *(wataseru) mono no*: = *keredomo*; more characteristic of written Japanese. ❖ *tashizan hikizan*: note the listings of two items without punctuation or conjunctions throughout this sentence.

rishoku nado "such a thing as moneymaking where you might even need differential or integral calculus"

なりそうな利殖など、考えただけでも頭が痛くなる。だいいち、商人というのは固いのがいちばん、株だの相場だのに手を出して商売をおろそかにしたあげく、左前になって店を畳むはめになっては元も子もない……というわけで、金融機関とのお付き合いは今まで、阿佐ヶ谷駅前の銀行一本槍だった。

そんな私が、直木賞の賞金として大枚百万円もの現金を手にしたのは、去年の夏のことだ。現金も現金、ぱりっぱりの新札の一万円札が連続番号できっちり揃って、かどなんか裁ち落としたばっかりという感じでとんがっている。

直木賞の賞金が百万円ということは知っていたが現金でいただけるとは思わず、受賞式では振込み通知書かなんかを受け取るだけだろうと思っていたか

• *kangaeta dake de mo atama ga itaku naru* "just the thought of it gives me a headache" • *daiichi* "first of all" • *shōnin to iu no wa katai no ga ichiban* "the safe and steady [lit., 'the tight,' as in 'tightfisted'] is foremost for a merchant" • *kabu dano sōba dano ni te o dashite [dasu]* "trying one's hand at stock or speculation" • *shōbai o orosoka ni shita ageku* "the upshot of neglecting one's own business" • *hidarimae ni natte* "fall flat on one's face" • *mise o tatamu hame ni natte [naru] wa* "be forced to close up (lit., 'fold up') shop" • *moto mo ko mo nai* "one loses both principal and interest" • *to iu wake de* "which is the reason why" • *kin'yū-kikan to no otsukiai wa* "my associations with financial institutions" • *ima made* "up to now" • *Asagaya ekimae no ginkō ippon-yari datta* "the bank in front of Asagaya station was my one and only stop" • *sonna watashi ga* "that being the kind of person I am, I (lit., 'that kind of I')" • *Naoki-shō no shōkin toshite* "as the prize money for the Naoki Prize" • *taimai hyakuman-en mo no genkin o* "the huge sum of ¥1 million in cash" • *te ni shita [suru] no wa* "(when) I got (lit., 'got in hand')" • *kyonen no natsu no koto da* "was summer of last year" • *genkin mo genkin* "it was hard cash" • *paripari no shinsatsu no ichiman-en-satsu ga renzoku-bangō de kitchiri sorotte [sorou]* "the crisp, new ¥10,000 bills were perfectly aligned in consecutive numbers" • *kado nanka* "the

❖ *narisō*: verb stem + *sō* = be likely to ~ , seem ~ . ❖ *kangaeta dake de mo*: a set expression. ❖ *kabu da no sōba da no*: equivalent to *to ka ~ to ka*; *darō ~ darō*. ❖ *te o dashite (dasu)*: lit., "to put out or extend one's hand." ❖ *(shita) ageku*: after -ing, when the outcome is unfavorable. ❖ *hidarimae ni natte (naru)*: lit., "to become left-in-front," from the custom of arranging the front fold of a kimono left over right for the deceased. ❖ *~ hame ni naru*: lit., "to become a wainscot," that is, wooden paneling firmly fixed to a wall (and thus not easily moved); be reduced to ~, be forced to ~ . ❖ *moto mo ko mo nai*: lit., "to lose both principal and interest," but as a general figure of speech, to lose everything, the whole kit and caboodle. Here the literal and figurative meanings both apply. ❖ *to iu wake de*: a common colloquial transitional phrase; here *wake* has its original meaning of "reason," in contrast to its nominalizing function elsewhere in this essay. ❖ *ippon yari*: a common idiom meaning "one spear"; i.e., one's only resource. ❖ *sonna watashi ga*: emphasis thrown on "I" to contrast the description preceding with that which follows. ❖ *natsu no koto*: here *koto* is synonymous with *dekigoto* (something that happened). ❖ *genkin mo genkin*: a common rhetorical device to emphasize nouns: *shinpin mo shinpin* "it's brand new (新品; something new)." ❖ *bakkari*: = *bakari*; the doubling of the consonant (characteristic of the spoken language) adds emphasis (note also *parippari* = *paripari*). ❖ *omowazu*. = *omowanaide*, from classical Japanese. ❖ *furikomi*: from the verb *furikomu* ("to transfer"); personal checks are little used in Japan, whereas the transfer of funds by wire to a savings account is common.

---

corners and all" • *tachiotoshita [tachiotosu] bakkari [bakari] to iu kanji de tongatte [tongaru] iru* "were sharply pointed as if they had just been cut (at the government mint)" • *Naoki-shō no shōkin ga hyakuman-en to iu koto wa shitte [shiru] ita ga* "I knew that the money for the Naoki Prize was ¥1 million, but" • *genkin de itadakeru to wa omowazu* "I had no idea that I could receive it in cash" • *jushō-shiki de wa* "at the award ceremony" • *furikomi-tsūchi-sho ka nanka o uketoru dake darō to omotte ita kara* "since I thought I would just receive something like a notification slip of payment by bank transfer"

らビックリした。

ビックリなんてしていないもんね、百万円くらいの現金なんか持ち慣れているもんね、という顔をしたかったが、背広の内ポケットに無造作らしく突っ込んだ封筒に、さすが百万円の厚みと迫力で受賞パーティの間じゅうワイシャツ越しに私の乳首を刺激しつづけられては、とてもそんな顔はできない。うれしさ半分、心配半分でようやく自宅へ帰り、まずは神棚に上げようと思ったが我が家には神棚がないので、とりあえず本棚の上に置いて考えた。

問題は、この百万円の使い途である。

この百万円を何に使うかである。

この百万円はタダの百万円ではない。

直木賞の賞金の百万円なのだから、それにふさわ

• *bikkuri shita* "I was surprised; caught by surprise" • *bikkuri nante shite inai mon ne ~ to iu kao o* "having a 'Hey, I'm not surprised' look on my face" • *hyakuman-en kurai no genkin nanka mochinarete [motsu + nareru] iru mon ne to iu kao o shitakatta ga* "I wanted to look as if I were used to carrying around sums like a million yen in cash, but" • *sebiro no uchi-poketto ni* "into the inside breast pocket of my suit" • *muzō-sa rashiku [rashii]* "in a casual, offhand way" • *tsukkonda [tsukkomu] fūtō ni sasuga hyakuman-en no atsumi to hakuryoku de* "the envelope thrust (into my pocket) had the thickness and impact one would expect of one million yen" • *jushō-pāti no aida-jū* "all through the award ceremony party" • *waishatsu-goshi ni watashi no chikubi o shigeki shitsuzuke-rarete [suru + tsuzukeru] wa* "with it pressing on my nipple through my shirt" • *totemo sonna kao wa dekinai* "I couldn't achieve that look at all" • *ureshi-sa hanbun, shinpai hanbun de [de aru]* "half happy and half anxious" • *yōyaku jitaku e kaeri [kaeru]* "at last I arrive home" • *mazu wa kamidana ni ageyō to omotta ga* "first of all I thought I would put it before the family Shinto shrine, but" • *waga-ie ni wa kamidana ga nai no de* "since there is no family shrine in our house" • *toriaezu* "for the time being" • *hondana no ue ni oite kangaeta* "I put it on the bookshelf and thought about it" • *mondai wa, kono hyakuman-en no tsukaimichi de*

❖ *shite inai mon ne*: *mon* = *mono*; when following a statement of feeling or fact, *mono* adds a slight note of subjective emphasis. ❖ *narete iru mon ne*: here *mon* (= *mono*) is giving the reason for the statement in the previous clause (*shite inai mon ne*). ❖ *sasuga*: in this sense used when one's expectations are confirmed; often followed by *ni*. ❖ *shigeki shitsuzukerarete*: stem + *tsuzuku* = continue -ing. ❖ *totemo ~ dekinai*: *totemo* is modifying the verb. ❖ *kamidana*: lit., "god shelf"; traditionally, Japanese houses have small Shinto shrines where offerings of food, flowers, etc. are made. ❖ *ageyō to omotta*: *-ō/yō to omou* = I thought I might ~ .

---

aru "the problem was how to use this one million yen" • *kono hyaku-man-en o nani ni tsukau ka de aru* "it was what to use this one million yen for" • *kono hyakuman-en wa tada no hyakuman-en de wa nai* "this one million yen was not just any old one million yen" • *Naoki-shō no shōkin no hyakuman-en da kara* "since this was the Naoki Prize money one million yen"

しい使い方をしなければならない。　私は腕を組んで考えた。

友人の小説家の高橋源一郎は、三島賞の賞金で競馬に行った。賞金をそっくりつぎ込んで馬券を買い、ぜんぶスッてしまったという記事が写真雑誌に載った。あれはあれでカッコいいが、商店街の小説で直木賞を戴いた私には似合わない。

次の小説の取材を兼ねて海外旅行にでも行くか？

いやいや、同時受賞の笹倉明氏ならそれもいいが、私にはやっぱり似合わない。友人知人とぱあっと飲みに行くといっても私は酒は飲めないし、オクサンに何かプレゼントというのも柄じゃない。息子と娘はそれぞれ下心があるらしくやたらとすりよってくるが、そんな甘い親でもない。

• *sore ni fusawashii tsukaikata o shinakereba naranai* "it must used in a suitable way" • *watashi wa ude o kunde [kumu] kangaeta* "I folded my arms and thought" • *yūjin no shōsetsu-ka no Takahashi Gen'ichirō wa* "my friend the novelist Takahashi Gen'ichirō" • *Mishima-shō no shōkin de* "with the money from the Mishima Prize" • *keiba ni itta [iku]* "he went to the race track" • *shōkin o sokkuri tsugikonde [tsugikomu]* "using up all the prize money" • *baken o kai [kau]* "he bet on the horses (lit., 'he bought horse tickets')" • *zenbu sutte [suru] shimatta* "he blew it all" • *to iu kiji ga shashin-zasshi ni notta [noru]* "an article to that effect appeared in a pictorial magazine" • *are wa are de kakko [kakkō] ii ga* "that is great for him, but" • *shōten-gai no shōsetsu-ka de Naoki-shō o itadaita [itadaku] watashi ni wa niawanai [niau]* "it doesn't suit (someone like) me who won the Naoki Prize for a novel about a small shopping district (lit., 'who is a small-shopping-district novelist')" • *tsugi no shōsetsu no shuzai o kanete [kaneru]* "combining it with research for my next novel" • *kaigai-ryokō ni de mo iku ka?* "how about going on a trip abroad?" • *iya-iya*: "oh, no" • *dōji-jushō no Sasakura Akira-shi nara sore mo ii ga* "that might be all right for my fellow prize winner Sasakura Akira, but" • *watashi ni wa yappari [yahari] niawanai* "that wouldn't, after all, suit someone like me" • *yūjin-chijin to pātto nomi ni iku to itte mo* "as for

❖ *sokkuri*: = the whole thing as it is. ❖ *sutte shimatta*: from *suru* (to scrape, grate; by extension "to lose all one's money"), with a slangish flavor; the helping verb *shimau* adds emphasis. ❖ *are wa are de*: lit., "that by itself"; *kore*, *sore*, and other nouns can be substituted; this phrase indicates that one's evaluation is conditional on time, circumstance, etc. ❖ *kakko ii*: *kakko* = *kakkō* (lit., "fine form"); colloquial for "great, out-of-this-world, cool." ❖ *shōten-gai no shōsetsu*: the novel for which Nejime received the Naoki Prize (*Kōenji junjō shōten-gai*) is about a district of small shops in Tokyo. ❖ *kaigai-ryokō ni de mo*: *de mo* here indicates possibilities other than the trip abroad, possibly translated as "a trip abroad, let's say." ❖ *iku ka?*: English exclamation points and question marks are sometimes used in non-formal writing. ❖ *iya-iya*: a duplication of *iya*, which likewise denies what someone has said or what oneself has said or thought. ❖ *pātto*: from *patto*; the lengthening of the vowel adds emphasis, in this case the spending of the money in one grand splurge. ❖ *gara ja nai*: (*gara* = "character, status, class"); the phrase ("ill-suited to one's character or ability") is idiomatic. ❖ *aru rashiku*: verb + *rashii* = it appears ~ . ❖ *yatara*: followed by *to* or *ni*, means "excessively, like crazy, like nobody's business." ❖ *amai oya*: *amai* (primarily, "sweet"), in the sense of being overly indulgent or generous.

---

going out drinking in a big way with friends and acquaintances" • *watashi wa sake wa nomenai [nomu] shi* "I'm not much of a drinker (lit., 'can't drink')" and • *okusan ni nani ka purezento to iu no mo gara ja nai* "getting some present for the wife is not my style either" • *musuko to musume wa sorezore shitagokoro ga aru rashiku* "my son and daughter seemed each to have designs (lit., 'under heart') on it" • *yatara to suriyotte [suriyoru] kuru ga* "have all of a sudden come sidling up to me, but" • *sonna amai oya de mo nai* "I'm not that soft a touch as a parent"

困った困ったと頭を抱え、ああでもないこうでもないと賞金の使い途を考えているうちに一週間がたった。その一週間のうちに、ああ、なんということか、本棚に上げた百万円は、気がつくと九十四万円に減っていたのだった。

もちろん減らしたのは私である。

この百万円を有意義に使わなくてはと考えながら、人と会うのでちょっと一枚、財布が淋しいのでとりあえず二枚という按配で一枚抜き二枚抜き、一週間たったらだいじなだいじな百万円を、六万円も使い込んでいたというわけである。

私はあせった。こんなふうに使っていては、直木賞の賞金が三ヶ月でなくなってしまう。これではいけない。ぜんぜん有意義ではない。こんなことでは、

• *komatta komatta to atama o kakae [kakaeru]* "holding my head in my hands and thinking, what a pickle" • *ā de mo nai kō de mo nai to* "rejecting one (plan) after another (lit., 'that isn't it, this isn't it')" • *shōkin no tsukaimichi o kangaete iru uchi ni* "while thinking of how to use the prize money" • *isshūkan ga tatta [tatsu]* "one week went by" • *sono isshūkan no uchi ni* "during that week" • *ā, nan to iu koto ka* "boy, what a mess" • *hondana ni ageta hyakuman-en wa* "the one million yen on the bookshelf" • *ki ga tsuku to* "when I noticed" • *kyūjūyonman-en ni hette [heru] ita no datta* "it had decreased to ¥940,000" • *mochiron herashita [herasu] no wa watashi de aru* "of course, it was I who decreased (reduced) it" • *kono hyakuman-en o yūigi ni tsukawanakute wa [= tsukawanakute wa naranai] to kangaenagara* "while thinking that I must use this one million yen in a meaningful way" • *hito to au no de chotto ichi-mai* "(I'll take) just one bill since I'm meeting someone" • *saifu ga sabishii no de toriaezu ni-mai* "(I'll take) two bills for the moment since my wallet is getting low (lit., 'lonely')" • *to iu anbai de ichimai-nuki [nuku] nimai-nuki* "in that way I took out one, (then) two" • *isshūkan tattara* "after one week" • *daiji na daiji na hyakuman-en o, rokuman-en mo tsukaikonde ita* "¥60,000 was used up out of that all-important one million yen" • *to iu wake de aru* "it turned out that ~ " • *watashi wa asetta* "I

❖ *komatta to*: common exclamation when facing a mild problem, always in the *-ta* form; repeated for effect. *To* would ordinarily be followed by *omotte*, *kangaete* or another verb, but which are commonly elided. ❖ *atama o kakae*: *atama o kakaeru* (lit., "to hold one's head" = to tear one's hair out) does not need to be taken literally. ❖ *tsukawanakute wa*: a contraction of *tsukawanakute wa ikenai [or naranai]*. ❖ *saifu ga sabishii*: idiomatic; *sabishii* often refers to human emotions, but can also refer to things that look desolate (e.g., *sabishii fūkei* "a bleak landscape"). ❖ *daiji na daiji na*: repeated for effect. ❖ *tsukaikonde*: *tsukaikomu* = to spend more than expected. ❖ *konna fū ni tsukatte ite wa*: = *kono tsukaikata shite ikeba*.

---

got fidgety; got in a sweat (lit., 'became impatient') • *konna fū ni tsukatte ite wa* "using it in this fashion" • *Naoki-shō no shōkin ga sankagetsu de nakunatte shimau* "the money from the Naoki Prize will be used up in three months" • *kore de wa ikenai* "this won't do" • *zenzen yūigi de wa nai* "this is not meaningful (usage of the money) at all"

直木賞の賞金をくださった直木三十五先生に申し訳ない。漫然と使ってしまった六万円を何とか元へ戻して、元どおりの百万円を直木賞にふさわしい使い方で使わなくてはならない。

そう考えた私は、残った九十四万円をさっそく近くの銀行に預金した。預金をすれば利息がつく。利息がつけば、九十四万円は百万円になる。

ところがところが、銀行のパンフレットをよく読むと、普通預金の金利は一年でわずか1％ちょっとだというではないか。九十四万円が百万円になって戻ってくるのに、これでは何年かかるかわかったものではない。

中学時代の同級生で今や売れっ子の経済評論家・海江田万里に相談したい心境になったが、たかが九

• *konna koto de wa, Naoki-shō no shōkin o kudasatta Naoki Sanjūgo sensei ni mōshiwake nai* "with things going like this, I'd never be able to raise my head in front of (justify myself to) the giver of the Naoki Prize, Naoki Sanjūgo (*mōshiwake nai* = to have no excuses)" • *manzen to tsukatte shimatta rokuman-en o nan to ka moto e modoshite [modosu]* "to restore the aimlessly (randomly) spent ¥60,000 somehow or other" • *moto-dōri no hyakuman-en o* "the restored one million yen" • *Naoki-shō ni fusawashii tsukaikata de tsukawanakute wa naranai* "I must use it in a way befitting the Naoki Prize" • *sō kangaeta watashi wa* "so thinking, I" • *nokotta kyūjūyonman-en o* "the remaining ¥940,000" • *sassoku chikaku no ginkō ni yokin shita* "I deposited right away in a nearby bank" • *yokin o sureba* "if you put it in a savings account" • *risoku ga tsuku* "it earns interest" • *risoku ga tsukeba [tsuku]* "if it earns interest (lit., 'if interest accrues')" • *kyūjūyonman-en wa hyakuman-en ni naru* "¥940,000 will turn into ¥1 million" • *tokoroga tokoroga* "however, however" • *ginkō no panfuretto o yoku yomu to* "if you take a good look at the bank leaflet (pamphlet)" • *futsū-yokin no kinri wa ichinen de* "in one year, the interest for an ordinary savings account" • *wazuka ichipāsento chotto da to iu de wa nai ka* "it says, is only a little over 1%, doesn't it" • *kyūjūyonman-en ga hyakuman-en ni natte modotte kuru no ni* "in order for ¥940,000 to

❖ *tokoroga tokoroga*: repeated for effect. ❖ *1% chotto*: *chotto* after a figure means "a little more than." ❖ *wakatta mono de wa nai*: an idiomatic expression stressing the impossibility of knowing. ❖ *urekko*: lit., "a person who is selling well." ❖ *Kaieda*: later elected to the House of Representatives.

turn back into ¥1 million" • *kore de wa nannen kakaru ka wakatta mono de wa nai* "at this (rate) who knows how many years it will take" • *chūgaku-jidai no dōkyū-sei de [de aru]* "a classmate of mine from middle school days" • *ima ya* "right now" • *urekko no keizai-hyōron-ka Kaieda Banri ni* "the much-in-demand economic commentator Kaieda Banri" • *sōdan shitai shinkyō ni natta ga* "I felt like consulting (lit., 'came into the state of mind of wanting to consult'), but"

十四万円で忙しい海江田を呼び出すのも気が引ける。

何とかもっと早く、一年くらいで賞金を元に戻す方法はないか。テレビで宣伝している中国ファンドはどうか。トップとかエースとかいうのはどうだろうか。何とかファンドという、「昨年度実績年利15％」などというスゴイ文句のついた証券会社のチラシがポストに入っていたが、それにしてみようか。

とはいえ、銀行としかお付き合いしたことのない私には証券会社は敷居が高い。それより、モノ書きが小説のことを考えずに利息のことばかり考えていては、直木三十五先生にもっと申し訳ない。考えれば考えるほどどうしたらいいかわからなくなって、わからなくなるほど何もする気がな

- *takaga kyūjūyonman-en de* "about a trifling ¥940,000" • *isogashii Kaieda o yobidasu no mo* "going so far as to summon (call up, see, meet on serious business) the busy Kaieda" • *ki ga hikeru* "can't bring myself to; feel a reluctance to (lit., 'the spirit withdraws')" • *nan to ka motto hayaku, ichinen kurai de* "somehow (to do it) more quickly, in about a year" • *shōkin o moto ni modosu hōhō wa nai ka* "isn't there some way of restoring the prize money to its original condition?" • *terebi de senden shite iru chūgoku-fando wa dō ka* "how about the Chūgoku Fund advertised on TV?" • *Toppu to ka Ēsu to ka iu no wa dō darō ka* "how about the one called Top or Ace or the like" • *nan to ka fando to iu* "the something or other fund" • *"sakunen-do jisseki nenri jūgo-pasento nado* "'an actual annual interest of 15% in the last fiscal year' etc." • *to iu sugoi monku no [= ga] tsuita shōken-gaisha no chirashi ga* "a flyer from a securities firm with such astounding catchphrases as" • *posuto ni haitte ita ga* "was in my mailbox, and" • *sore ni shite miyō ka* "maybe I should try that" • *to wa ie [iu]* "and yet" • *ginkō to shika otsukiai shita koto no nai watashi ni wa* "for me, who has never dealt with anything but banks" • *shōken-gaisha wa shikii ga takai* "a securities firm is out of my league" • *sore yori* "more importantly (lit., 'more than that')" • *monokaki ga shō-setsu no koto o kangaezu ni risoku no koto bakari kangaete ite wa* "a

❖ *takaga*: an adverb meaning "at most, as little as, as trifling a matter as." ❖ *nantoka fando*: used with a noun, *nantoka* can replace a noun not remembered, unimportant, or not worth mentioning. ❖ *chirashi*: one-page printed flyers advertising real estate companies, supermarkets, etc.; often placed in personal mailboxes or delivered with daily newspapers. ❖ *shite miyō ka*: *-te* + *miru* = try out -ing, do ~ and see how it works. ❖ *to wa ie*: lit., "having said that"; indicates second thoughts about something. ❖ *shika ~ koto no nai*: *shika* + negative = *dake* + positive. ❖ *shikii ga takai*: lit., "the threshold or doorsill is high"; indicates feelings of reluctance or hesitation. ❖ *monokaki*: note the use of the older and broader word for "writer" rather than the newer and more specific *shōsetsu-ka* (novelist). ❖ *kangaezu ni*: = *kangaenai de*. ❖ *kangaereba kangaeru hodo*: *-eba/-reba ~ -u/-ru hodo* = the more one ~ , the more ~ .

writer thinking only about interest and not thinking about his novels" • *Naoki Sanjūgo-sensei ni motto mōshiwake nai* "I would find it even more difficult to justify myself to Naoki Sanjūgo" • *kangaereba kangaeru hodo dō shitara ii no ka wakaranaku natte* "the more I thought about it the more I didn't know what to do" • *wakaranaku nareba naru hodo nani mo suru ki ga naku natte* "the more I didn't know what to do the less I felt like doing anything"

くなって、私は何もしないことにした。

以来八ヶ月、株は大暴落となり、円はますます安くなり、何だか知らないがあとのひとつも安くなって、今は「トリプル安」の大嵐が吹いているらしい。

しかし、私の直木賞の賞金は、銀行の普通預金口座でのんびり昼寝している。あれからカードでだいぶ引き出してしまったけど、いったいいくら残っているのだろうか。

………………一九九〇年四月十五日

• *watashi wa nani mo shinai koto ni shita* "I decided not to do anything"
• *irai hakkagetsu* "since then, for eight months" • *kabu wa daibōraku to nari [naru]* "stocks have plummeted" • *en wa masumasu yasuku nari* "the yen has fallen more and more (against the dollar; lit., 'gotten cheaper')" • *nan da ka shiranai ga ato no hitotsu mo yasuku natte* "I don't know (exactly) what, but one more has fallen (gotten cheap), too" • *ima wa* "now" • *"toripuru-yasu" no ōarashi ga fuite (fuku) iru rashii* "it seems that the tempest of the 'triple fall (cheapness)' is blowing" • *shikashi* "however" • *watashi no Naoki-shō no shōkin wa* "my money from the Naoki Prize" • *ginkō no futsū-yokin-kōza de* "in an ordinary savings account at the bank" • *nonbiri hirune shite iru* "is peacefully napping" • *are kara* "since then" • *kādo de* "using a bank cash card" • *daibu hikidashite shimatta kedo* "I have withdrawn quite a bit of money from it, and" • *ittai ikura nokotte iru darō ka* "I wonder exactly how much is left anyway"

❖ *suru ki ga nakunatte*: ~ *ki ga nakunaru* = lose the desire to ~ ; ~ *ki ni naru* = feel like -ing. ❖ *shinai koto ni shita*: ~ *koto ni suru* = decide to ~ . ❖ *fuite iru rashii*: ~ *rashii* = it seems (I heard) that ~ . ❖ *ittai*: an intensifier with the meaning "what in the world, why on earth."

Sakura Momoko

Born in Shizuoka Prefecture in 1965, Sakura Momoko is the creator of the best-selling *Chibi Maruko-chan*. This autobiographical *manga* about elementary students in a regional city in the 1970s became a hit with young women and others and was also made into a popular animated television series. Sakura's first book of light essays, *Momo no kanzume*, was a runaway bestseller and was followed by two additional best-selling volumes: *Saru no koshikake* and *Tai no okashira*.

Sakura's essay here, from *Momo no kanzume*, is a light-hearted account of her ill-fated attempt to work at a nine-to-five job in an office.

First published in *Shōsetsu subaru*. Copyright 1990 by Sakura Momoko. The essay also appears in the author's book *Momo no kanzume*. Reprinted by permission of Shūeisha and the author.

宴会用の女

さくらももこ

人間には『向き』『不向き』があるものだ。私は
OLをやってみて、つくづくそう思った。

以前なら、友達が「私って、OLに向いてないみ
たい」などと言うのを聞いて　　"そんなのワガママ
よ、OLなんて学校に通うのと同じで、言われたと
おりにやってりゃいいんだから、向き不向きなんて
ないんじゃないの"と傲慢にも思っていたが、とん
でもない思い違いであった。

両親の反対を押し切って上京した私は、某出版社
に就職した。出版社といっても、ファッション誌や
情報誌等の華やかな本を作るのではなく、政府刊行

- *enkai-yō no onna* "a woman for party use" • *ningen ni wa "muki" "fu-muki" ga aru mono da* "there is such a thing as 'suitability' and 'unsuitability' in human beings" •*watashi wa ō-eru o yatte mite* "having tried my hand as an OL" • *tsukuzuku sō omotta [omou]* "I was fully convinced of it" • *izen nara* "before that (lit., 'if before')" • *tomodachi ga "watashi tte, ō-eru ni muite 'nai mitai" nado to iu no o kiite [kiku]* "hearing a friend say something like, 'I don't seem suited to being an OL'" • *sonna no wagama-ma yo* "you're just being spoiled (lit., 'that's just being self-centered')" • *ō-eru nante gakkō ni kayou no to onaji de [de aru]* "being an OL is the same as going to school" • *iwareta tōri ni yatte rya [yatte ireba] ii n' da kara* "since all you have to do is do what you're told" • *muki fu-muki nante nai n' ja nai no [=ka]* "there is no such thing as suited or unsuited" • *to gōman ni mo omotte ita ga* "I was arrogant enough to believe, but" • *tonde mo nai omoichigai de atta* "it was a terrible mistake (lit., 'misapprehension')" • *ryōshin no hantai o oshikitte [oshikiru]* "overcoming my parents' objections (lit., 'opposition')" • *jōkyō shita watashi wa* "coming to Tokyo, I" • *bō-shuppan-sha ni shūshoku shita* "I found a job at a certain publishing company" • *shuppan-sha to itte mo* "though I say 'a publisher'" • *fasshon-shi ya jōhō-shi nado no hanayaka na hon o tsukuru no de wa naku* "it did not produce showy publications like fashion maga-

❖ *"muki" "fumuki"*: the brackets are generally equivalent to English quotation marks or italics. ❖ *ga aru mono da*: following a verb or adjective, *mono* indicates that the speaker is making (stressing) an objective judgement about a state of affairs: e.g., *yo no naka wa kō iu mono da* ("This is the way of the world"). ❖ OL: "office ladies"; the young women sometimes referred to as "office flowers" (*shokuba no hana*), who make photocopies, serve tea, and do clerical work until quitting before getting married in their late twenties. ❖ *yatte mite*: *-te* + *miru* = try doing ~ . Here, the past is in question, so the translation is "having tried doing ~," with the meaning of "on the basis of my experience of having worked as an OL." *Yaru* here = to carry out an action, in which sense it is largely synonymous with *suru*, but which cannot be replaced by it here. ❖ *watashi tte*: "as for me (or, speaking of myself, I)"; can be paraphrased as *watashi to iu ningen wa* or *watashi to iu no wa* (see also the largely synonymous *OL to wa* later). ❖ *wagamama yo*: *yo* here is feminine; a man would more likely say, *wagamama da yo*. ❖ *muki fumuki nante*: *nante* = *nanka, nado wa*, in a belittling reference; similar to English "and their ilk," but colloquial. ❖ *yatterya*: a common colloquial contraction of *yatte ireba*. ❖ *ja nai no*: *no* often appears in questions (more often by women) in place of *ka*. ❖ *tonde mo nai*: stresses the absurdity of something; often used independently in denial as an exclamation. ❖ *jōkyō shita*: one always goes "up" to Tokyo as the capital regardless of physical direction. ❖ *bō-shuppan-sha*: *bō-* is added to nouns for the meaning of "a certain ~ ." ❖ *shuppan-sha to itte mo*: *to itte mo* indicates that some qualification will follow (i.e., you may think a publisher is a glamorous place to work, but actually …). ❖ *jōhō-shi*: i.e., magazines like *Pia* and *Hanako*, which give listings for current films, concerts, plays, etc. as well as news on the latest trends in fashion, foods, interior furnishings, etc. ❖ *hon*: here, includes magazines as well as books

zines or information magazines"

物ばかりを作る、きわめて地味な職場であった。

私は営業課に配属された。営業課といっても、外回りして「これを買って下さい」などという仕事は全て男性社員がやり、女性は資料の整理や注文書の伝票を機械にインプットしたりする、完全な事務作業であった。

私の班は男性三名、女性五名の計八名で活動していた。女の先輩は皆気立てが良く、とても親切だったのだが、男三名は良くなかった。

特に私の横にいる男は30歳前後でメガネをかけ、実に貧相で下品な風貌であった。この男をこの先"先輩"と呼び、慕わなければならないのかと思うと、労働意欲が蒸発していく気がしたが、一応「どうぞよろしくお願いします」とあいさつした。

- *seifu-kankōbutsu bakari o tsukuru, kiwamete jimi na shokuba de atta* "it was a very conservative workplace, producing nothing but government publications" • *watashi wa eigyō-ka ni haizoku sareta* "I was assigned to the sales section" • *eigyō-ka to itte mo* "though I say 'the sales section'" • *sotomawari shite* "making the rounds (of business outside the company)" • *"Kore o katte kudasai" nado to iu shigoto wa* "work such as saying, 'Would you buy this'" • *subete dansei-shain ga yari [yaru]* "is all done by male employees" • *josei wa ~, kanzen na jimu-sagyō de atta* "the women (employees) ~ had completely clerical (office) work" • *shiryō no seiri ya chūmon-sho no denpyō o kikai ni inputto shitari suru* "doing things like organizing data and imputting order slips into machines" • *watashi no han wa* "my unit" • *dansei sanmei, josei gomei no kei hachimei de katsudō shite ita* "it operated with a total of eight people, three men and five women" • *onna no senpai wa mina kidate ga yoku [yoi]* "the women senior to me were all good-natured" • *totemo shinsetsu datta no da ga* "were very kind, but" • *otoko sanmei wa yoku nakatta* "the three men were not so good" • *toku ni watashi no yoko ni iru otoko wa* "in particular, the man (whose desk was) next to me" • *sanjussai zengo de [de aru]* "was around thirty years old" • *megane o kake [kakeru]* "he wore glasses" • *jitsu ni hinsō de [de*

❖ *jimi na shokuba*: *jimi* is used in a wide variety of contexts to refer to the quiet and conservative; the antonym is *hade* (flashy, gaudy). ❖ *input-to shitari suru*: *-tari suru* indicates that this is only one example of things they do. ❖ *han*: workers in Japanese offices are often divided into such permanent work teams. ❖ *senpai*: people senior to one in age or experience; those junior are *kōhai*. ❖ *kono otoko*: note the use of *otoko* throughout for the "seedy person" rather than *dansei* or *hito* (which would raise the level of politeness); i.e., the author keeps her references to the man at the lowest possible level, not resorting to the more polite forms thought to be characteristic of women in general. ❖ *shitawanakereba*: *shitau* = to follow, learn from, and emulate a respected teacher or master; this somewhat high-flown word is employed for (exaggerated) effect. Below, see also *imawashii*, *kakugo*, *shirei*, *taiki*, *jinsei*, *kyōgaku*, *sangeki*, *zekkyō*, and *kyōfun*. ❖ *dōzo yoroshiku onegai shimasu*: set expression when entering a relationship; in brackets to show the author said nothing more to curry favor.

aru] gehin na fūbō de atta "he was truly seedy and coarse-looking" • *kono otoko o kono saki "senpai" to yobi [yobu], shitawanakereba [shitau] naranai no ka to omou to* "when I thought how I would shortly have to learn at the knees of (lit., 'to respect and emulate') this person and call him *senpai* • *rōdō-iyoku ga jōhatsu shite iku ki ga shita ga* "I felt my zeal for work disappearing (lit., 'evaporating'), but" • *ichiō "dōzo yoroshiku onegai shimasu" to aisatsu shita* "anyhow (for the time being), I made the (conventional) greeting, saying, 'I would appreciate any help you might give me.'"

貧相で下品なその男は、私のあいさつなどどうでもいいという様子で「ああ」と言い、そのまま仕事を続けていた。横顔をよく見ると、数本鼻毛が伸びていた。

この会社には、実に忌まわしい暗黙の掟がある。いや、規則では出勤時刻七時半という規則である。八時四十五分までに来れば良いという事になっているのだ。ところが社長が〝年寄りの早起き〟で、六時頃出社してくるため、部下も倣って早起きをし、平社員も七時半を過ぎての出社は気まずくてできないのである。

上京したばかりの頃の私は、とにかく出費をできるだけ抑えて暮らそうと思っていたので、毎朝五時に起きて弁当を作った。OLとはこんなに辛いもの

• *hinsō de [de aru] gehin na sono otoko wa* "this seedy, coarse person" • *watashi no aisatsu nado dō de mo ii to iu yōsu de [de aru]* "acting as if he could care less about anything like a greeting from me" • *"aa" to ii [iu]* "he says, 'Yeah'" • *sono mama shigoto o tsuzukete ita* "he went on with his job (without further notice of me)" • *yokogao o yoku miru to* "when I took a close look at him in profile" • *sūhon hanage ga nobite ita* "(I noticed that) several hairs were growing (lit., 'extending forth') from his nostrils" • *kono kaisha ni wa* "in this company" • *jitsu ni imawashii anmoku no okite ga aru* "there is a truly loathsome (lit., 'unlucky; ill-omened') unspoken law" • *shukkin-jikoku shichiji-han to iu kisoku de aru* "the regulations that work begins at 7:30" • *iya* "no (well, actually)" • *kisoku de wa* "according to the regulations" • *hachiji yonjūgo-fun made ni kureba [kuru] yoi* "it was all right to come by 8:45" • *to iu koto ni natte iru no da* "such is the way it was decided (arranged, set up)" • *tokoroga* "however" • *shachō ga "toshiyori no hayaoki" de* "the company president had the old person's (habit of) waking up early" • *rokuji-goro shussha shite kuru tame* "because he came to the office about 6:00" • *buka mo naratte [narau] hayaoki o shi [suru]* "his subordinates followed his example by also getting up early" • *hira-shain mo shichiji-han o sugite no shussha wa* "coming later than 7:30 for ordinary employees

❖ *dō de mo ii*: lit., "any way is all right"; set colloquial expression indicating that any way is all right or, in this case, one isn't interested. ❖ *aa*: can have various meanings (yes: oh!) according to intonation (here pronounced flatly); is in this case just a rude sound indicating he heard her. ❖ *okite*: a rule, regulation, or law established by custom in a group or small society (e.g., an island community); here the contrast is between the *okite* and the company regulations (*kisoku*). ❖ *iya*: a negative exclaimation to deny what someone else has said (『暑い？』『—、暑くない』 *"Atsui?" "Iya, atsuku nai"*) or, as here, to correct what one has just said. ❖ *to iu koto ni natte iru*: = it is established that; it has been decided that; it is supposed to be so-and-so. ❖ *shachō*: often used in place of a name or as a term of address. ❖ *buka*: lit., "under the *bu* [department]"; specifically those working in a department under a department head; generally, subordinates of a business leader. ❖ *hira-shain*: *hira-* adds the meaning "plain," "ordinary," or "common," indicating an employee in a non-managerial position; *hira* can stand by itself but has derogatory connotations. ❖ *kimazukute*: *kimazui* refers to an unpleasant or strained situation or to feelings of awkwardness or embarrassment; *mazui* has meanings like distasteful, poorly produced or done, and inconvenient. ❖ *dekiru dake*: set phrase meaning "as much as possible." ❖ *kurasō to omotte ita*: stem + *-ō/yō to omou/suru* = to try to ~ . ❖ *tsurai mono na no ka*: *mono* here reinforces the writer's emotional involvement and adds a sense of amazement.

as well" • *ki-mazukute dekinai no de aru* "made them feel so awkward that they couldn't do it" • *jōkyō shita bakari no koro no watashi wa* "I, who had just come to Tokyo" • *tonikaku* "in any event" • *shuppi o dekiru dake osaete [osaeru] kurasō [kurasu] to omotte ita no de* "since I thought I would try to live by keeping expenses down as much as possible (i.e., live as inexpensively as possible)" • *maiasa goji ni okite [okiru] bentō o tsukutta* "every morning I got up at 5:00 and made a box lunch" • *ō-eru to wa konna ni tsurai mono na no ka to, ~ naita mono de aru* "I used to cry, ~ how could being an OL be so tough"

なのかと、米を研ぎながら泣いたものである。

入社して一週間目頃、新入社員歓迎会が開かれる事になった。「そうかそうか、歓迎してくれるのか」と呑気に構えていたところ、「新人の皆さんには、全員一曲ずつ歌を披露してもらいますから、明日は覚悟しておいて下さい」との指令が下った。

歌……、私はこれまでに人前で歌った事なんて、幼稚園の遠足のバスの中で死ぬほどイヤだったが『カエルのうた』をゲロゲロと歌った以外に一度もない。

泣き出しそうになっている私の肩をポンと叩き「キミ、短大にいた頃、みんなの前で漫才をやったんだってねェ。面白そうだから我が社で採用したんだよ。明日も期待しているからね」と、にこやかな

• *kome o toginagara* "while washing the rice (before cooking it)" • *nyūsha shite isshūkan-me goro* "in about the first week after joining the company" • *shinnyū-shain–kangei-kai ga hirakareru koto ni natta* "it was decided to have a welcoming party for new employees" • *"sō ka sō ka, kangei shite kureru no ka" to nonki ni kamaete ita tokoro* "just as I had blithely taken the stance that 'hey, wow, they're going to welcome us'" • *shinjin no mina-san ni wa* "all of the newcomers" • *zen'in ikkyoku-zutsu uta o hirō shite moraimasu kara* "since we will have (all of the newcomers) perform one song each" • *asu wa kakugo shite oite kudasai* "tomorrow please be prepared (for the worst)" • *to no shirei ga kudatta [kudaru]* "the directive was issued that ~ " • *uta ...* "a song ..." • *watashi wa* "as for me" • *kore made ni hitomae de utatta [utau] koto nante* " my piddling experience in singing before people up to now" • *yōchi-en no ensoku no basu no naka de shinu hodo iya datta ga* "in the bus on a kindergarten school outing, but which I really hated (lit., 'was hateful to the point of dying')" • *"kaeru no uta" o gerogero to utatta igai ni ichido mo nai* "was the one and only time I croaked out the *Frog Song*" • *naki-dashisō ni natte iru watashi no kata o pon to tataki* "clapping me, who was on the verge of tears, on the shoulder" • *kimi* "you (informal)" • *tandai ni ita koro* "when you were in junior college" • *minna no mae de*

❖ *toginagara*: stem + *nagara* = while -ing. ❖ *naita mono*: here *mono* indicates habitual action. ❖ *kamaete ita tokoro*: *-ta* + *tokoro* = just as I was doing ~ . *Kamaeru* = to build, establish, take a stance, assume an attitude; note the contrast between the firmness of "stance" and the infirmity of "blithely." ❖ *uta*: Japanese parties often feature such amateur performances. ❖ *asu*: the *kanji* can also be read as *ashita*, which is more common in speech; *asu* is the recommended *jōyō kanji* reading. ❖ *kakugo shite oite*: *oku* indicates something done in preparation or in advance; *kakugo* here connotes both "preparing oneself mentally" and "resigning oneself to some unpleasantness," though the latter may not apply in all contexts. ❖ *ensoku*: most Japanese schools have class outings to historical sites or the like once or twice a year. ❖ *shinu hodo iya*: idiomatic expression; the *katakana* is for emphasis. ❖ *gerogero*: the sound frogs make, which appears in the song. ❖ *utatta igai ni ichido mo nai*: lit., "not once, aside from singing ~ ." ❖ *nakidashisō*: stem + *sō* = to look as if one would ~ ; see also *omoshirosō* below. ❖ *pon to tataki*: *pon to* refers to a single abrupt action such as clapping someone on the shoulder or putting money on the table in a grand gesture. ❖ *kimi*: "you (informal)," used generally among men to someone equal in status or age, someone younger, or a subordinate (though there are severe restrictions within these guidelines). Here, written in *katakana* to reproduce the sound for realistic effect, it shows the relative status of the newcomer and the entrenched assistant section chief. ❖ *manzai*: comic routines with two people. ❖ *wagasha*: *waga* can be added to certain nouns with the meaning "our." ❖ *kitai shite iru*: *kitai* is often used to indicate that one is looking forward to something or expecting great things of the other.

---

manzai o yatta n' datte nē "I hear that you did public (lit., 'in front of everyone') *manzai* performances" • *omoshirosō da kara* "because (you) seem interesting" • *wagasha de saiyō shita n' da yo* "we hired you at our company" • *asu mo kitai shite iru kara ne* "we're expecting great things of you tomorrow, too, so (prepare something good)" • *to, nikoyaka na kao de* "(so he said), with a smiling face"

顔で課長が通りすぎていった。私は、この会社の色
物担当用の女として雇われているのか……。
家路につく地下鉄の中でも、ずっと　"面白いか
ら採用した" という言葉だけが頭の中にゴトンゴト
ンと響いていた。
家に帰ってから、私は早速歌の練習を始めた。中
島みゆきの『極楽通りへいらっしゃい』というけだ
るい歌を、ボソボソと何十回もくり返し練習した。
六畳一間のアパートの壁は薄い。こんな、一人暮
らしの女のうす気味悪い歌声が、隣室に流れたら他
人にも迷惑がかかる、などといろいろ気を配りなが
ら部屋の片隅で背中を丸めながら歌い続け、夜が更ふ
けた。
翌日、仕事が終わってからいよいよ新入社員歓迎

• *kachō ga tōrisugite itta* "the section chief passed by me (clapping me
on the shoulder etc.)" • *kono kaisha no iromono-tantō-yō no onna toshite*
"as the woman to serve as the company entertainer (lit., 'the woman for
use as being in charge of entertainment')" • *yatowarete iru no ka … :*
"you mean I was hired (as …)" • *ieji ni tsuku chika-tetsu no naka de mo*
"even in the subway on the way home" • *zutto* "all the while" • *omoshiroi kara saiyō shita" to iu kotoba dake ga* "only the words, 'We hired
you because you're interesting'" • *atama no naka ni gotongoton to hibi-
ite [hibiku] ita* "reverberated in my head (lit., 'echoed with a clatter in
my head')" • *ie ni kaete [kaeru] kara* "after getting home" • *sassoku*
"right away" • *uta no renshū o hajimeta* "I started to practice singing" •
Nakajima Miyuki no "Nakajima Miyuki's (written and sung by her)" •
"Gokuraku-dōri e irasshai" "Drop by (lit., 'Come to') Paradise Street"* •
to iu kedarui uta o "the languorous song entitled ~ " • *bosoboso to* "in an
undertone" • *nan-jukkai mo kurikaeshi [kurikaesu] renshū shita* "I practiced by repeating it tens of times" • *rokujō-hitoma no apāto no kabe wa
usui* "the walls of a single-room, six-mat apartment are thin" • *konna,
hitori-gurashi no onna no usukimi-warui utagoe ga, rinshitsu ni nagare-
tara [nagareru]* "if this kind of eerie singing voice of a woman living
alone should carry to the room next door" • *tanin ni mo meiwaku ga*

❖ *kachō*: *kakari-chō* is the lowest rank of manager followed by *kachō* and *buchō*. Such terms are often used in place of the personal name or as a term of address. ❖ *iromono-tantō*: *tantō(-sha)* refers to the person in charge of something, but of course no company has an official *iromono-tantō-(sha)*. ❖ *gotongoton*: onomatopoeia for a train passing over rails. ❖ *Nakajima Miyuki*: singer and songwriter famous for depicting the darker side of life. ❖ *bosoboso*: onomatopoeia for whispering or talking in a low voice. ❖ *nanjukkai*: *nan* + number = in the tens, thousands, etc. (*nanbyaku* = hundreds; *nanzen* = thousands). ❖ *rokujō*: room sizes are generally designated in terms of number of *tatami* mats (one mat is approximately 6 ft. x 3 ft.). ❖ *meiwaku ga kakaru / meiwaku o kakeru*: be a nuisance, inconvenience someone; often used as a polite phrase before or after receiving a mild favor (*gomeiwaku deshō ga ...; meiwaku o kakete dōmo sumimasen deshita*). ❖ *nado to*: *nado* ("and so on") shows that there were possibilities other than the inconveniece to others; the *to* after *nado*, logically following *meiwaku ga kakaru*, is an abbreviation of *to iu yō ni* ("such things as inconvenience to others etc."); this usage of *to* (with the rest of the phrase understood: *to itte, to iu fū ni, to iu yō ni*) is seen throughout. ❖ *utaitsuzuke*: stem + *tsuzukeru* = continue -ing.

---

kakaru "it would be a bother to others, too (i.e., besides being a bother to me)" • *nado to iroiro ki o kubarinagara [kubaru]* "while worrying about this and that" • *heya no katasumi de* "in one corner of the room" • *senaka o marumenagara [marumeru] utaitsuzuke [utaitsuzukeru]*: "I continued singing while hunching over (i.e., she was not only singing in a small voice but also making her body as small as possible)" • *yo ga fuketa* "the night wore on" • *yokujitsu* "the next day" • *shigoto ga owatte [owaru] kara* "after work was over" • *iyoiyo shinnyū-shain kangei-kai ga hajimatta [hajimaru]* "the welcoming party for newcomers began at last"

会が始まった。会場は、社内の雑然とした一室で、仕事机の上に点々とビールやら酒やら簡単な食べ物等が置かれていた。

なんか、貧乏な家のクリスマス会という感じである。私は景気づけのためにビールをゴクゴク飲み、おとなしく自分の出番まで待機していた。

同期の仲間が次々指名され、楽しく自己紹介をし、歌っていく。皆、堂々としたものである。『走れコータロー』を歌って景気づける者もいて、場はかなり盛り上がっていた。

「さて、いよいよトリをとってもらうのはお待ちかね、さくらさんです。イェー」

泣きたくなるような軽い掛け声にあおられて、私は会場の中央に躍り出た。

• *kaijō wa, shanai no zatsuzen to shita isshitsu de [de aru]* "the site of the party was a cluttered room in the (office) building" • *shigoto-zukue no ue ni* "on (top of) a desk" • *tenten to* "(scattered) here and there" • *bīru yara sake yara kantan na tabemono nado ga okarete [oku] ita* "there was (lit., 'had been placed') beer and *sake* and simple food (i.e., little snacks) etc." • *nanka* "somehow; for some reason" • *binbō na ie no kurisumasu-kai to iu kanji de aru* "it had the look of a Christmas party at a needy household" • *keiki-zuke no tame ni* "in order to buck myself up" • *bīru o gokugoku nomi [nomu]* "I gulped down some beer" • *otonashiku [otonashii]* "quietly, meekly" • *jibun no deban made taiki shite ita* "I awaited my turn (to perform) (lit., 'I held myself in readiness for my turn')" • *dōki no nakama ga* "my fellow new employees" • *tsugitsugi ni shimei sare [sareru]* "were called upon one after another" • *tanoshiku jiko-shōkai o shi [suru]* "cheerfully introduced themselves" • *utatte iku* "they proceeded to sing [lit., 'they went and sang [in turn]')" • *mina dōdō to shita mono de aru* "they were all full of confidence" • *"Hashire Kōtarō" o utatte [utau]* "singing *Run, Kōtarō* (a song about a race horse)" • *keiki-zukeru mono mo ite [iru]* "there were those (singers) who livened things up" • *ba wa kanari moriagatte [moriagaru] ita* "the party (lit., 'the place') had become quite lively (lit., 'had risen up')" • *sate*

❖ *bīru yara sake yara*: *yara* is similar to *nado*: drinks like beer and *sake*.
❖ *gokugoku*: onomatopoeia for drinking something in gulps. ❖ *taiki*: = to hold oneself in readiness, as firefighters fully outfitted and waiting to go into action; this usage shows how nervous the author was while waiting for her turn. ❖ *dōki no nakama*: i.e., people hired at the same time as Sakura (most Japanese companies hire new employees at the beginning of April). ❖ *dōdō to shita mono*: *mono* here adds a note of emotional emphasis; the phrase could otherwise have been simply *dōdō to shite ita*. ❖ *ba wa*: *ba* ("place") has a number of meanings; here, the atmosphere or mood of a gathering. ❖ *sate*: often used at the beginning of remarks or when changing the subject. ❖ *tori o toru*: a phrase formerly used only among *yose* (a kind of vaudeville) entertainers for the most important entertainer who concludes the program.

"well now" • *iyo-iyo* "at last" • *tori o totte morau no wa* "appearing last but not least" • *omachikane [machikaneru]* "the person you have all been waiting for" • *Sakura-san desu* "here's Miss Sakura" • *iee* "hooray" • *nakitaku naru yō na karui kakegoe ni aorarete [aoru]* "spurred on by shouts so superficial (lit., 'light') that one wanted to cry" • *watashi wa kaijō no chūō ni odorideta [odorideru]* "I bound into the center of the room"

まずは夢中で自己紹介をし、かなりの笑いをとったので "フッ、よしよし私の実力なんてこんなもんよ" といい気になり、そのまま歌に突入した。「中島みゆきの『極楽通りへいらっしゃい』を歌います」と言ったとたん「いいぞー」等の歓声が湧き、歌い出すと共に手拍子が鳴り始めた。

♬「どこから来たの〜って
わたし〜が聞いた〜ら
慣れたフリし〜て
こたえ〜てね〜」

みんなニコニコ顔で聞いていたが、歌が二番にさしかかる頃、だんだん様子がおかしくなってきた。

♬「今日は何回頭下げた〜の
人からバカだって言われ〜たのォォ

• *mazu wa* "first of all" • *muchū de* "as if in a dream, frantically" • *jiko-shōkai o shi [suru]* "I introduced myself" • *kanari no warai o totta [toru] no de* "since I won a good deal of laughter" • *fu* "ha ha" • *yoshiyoshi* "alright" • *watashi no jitsuryoku nante konna mon yo to ii ki ni nari [naru]* "I started feeling pretty good (about myself): 'this is the real me (lit., "my true ability")'" • *sono mama uta ni totsunyū shita* "I plunged straight into the song" • *Nakajima Miyuki no "Gokuraku-dōri e irasshai" o utaimasu* "I'm going to sing "Drop by Paradise Street" by Nakajima Miyuki" • *to itta totan* "as soon as I said that" • *"ii zō" nado no kansei ga waki [waku]* "cheers of 'Great!' etc. broke out (lit., 'welled up')" • *utaidasu to tomo ni* "as soon as I started to sing" • *tebyōshi ga narihajimeta* "clapping in time to the beat began" • *doko kara kita nō [no] tte, watashī ga kiitāra [kiitara]* "when I asked you where you were from" • *nareta furi shīte [shite] kotaēte nē* "you answered in a practiced way" • *minna nikoniko-gao de kiite [kiku] ita ga* "everyone listened with smiles on their faces, but" • *uta ga niban ni sashikakaru koro* "about the time the song approached the second verse" • *dandan yōsu ga okashiku natte kita* "things started to get funny (lit., 'gradually got funny')" • *kyō wa* "today" • *nankai atama sagetā [sageta] no [= ka]* "how many times have you bowed (to your clients)" • *hito kara baka datte iwarēta [iware-*

✤ *fu*: a sound made to oneself when happy or self-satisfied, particularly as visually represented in *manga*. ✤ *yoshiyoshi*: shows self-satisfaction with oneself, as here, or with others when things are going well. ✤ *ii ki ni naru*: lit., "to get (or have) a good feeling"; here the meaning is to feel so good that it goes to one's head. ✤ *irasshai*: the imperative form of *irassharu* (come), not to be confused with *irasshaimase* ("welcome"). ✤ *itta totan*: *-ta totan* = as soon as something happened ~ then ~. ✤ *zō (zo)*: a rough, emphatic particle generally used by men; elongated for emphasis. ✤ *furi shite*: = to pretend to ~, as in *neta furi o suru* (pretend to be sleeping). ✤ *yōsu ga okashiku natte kita*: a set phrase meaning things turned bad (lit., "the situation started to get funny"). ✤ *atama (o) sageta*: i.e., humbling oneself in asking for an order, in apology for a delayed shipment, etc. ✤ *baka*: common in calling someone an idiot or stupid.

---

ta] nō [no] "(how many times) were you called 'a fool' by somebody"

なぐり返したぁぁい気持ちをためてェ

わたしィを笑い〜に来たんでしょ〜」

これはサラリーマンの悲しみを場末（ばすえ）の飲み屋の女

が慰める歌だったのだ。

内心〝しまった〟と思いながらあとには引けず、

うつむいてゆく男性社員の顔を見ながら、私は歌い

続けるしかなかった。

♬「幸せ不幸せ混ぜてあげるゥ

今夜は〜よ〜こそ〜

ここは極楽通り〜……」

あんなに盛り上がっていた場は一気に静まり、歌

い終わった私は地獄通りからやって来た不吉な女に

なっていた。針の筵（むしろ）を歩くような思いで席に戻り、

ひきつったままの顔でビールをゴクリと飲み干し

• *nagurikaeshitāi [kaeshitai] kimochi o tametē [tamete]* "having stored up the desire to hit back" • *watashī [watashi] o waraī [warai; warau] ni kita n' deshō* "you've probably come to laugh at me (i.e., take your frustrations out on me)" • *kore wa sararīman no kanashimi o basue no nomiya no onna ga nagusameru uta datta no da* "this was the song of a bar girl in an out-of-the-way drinking place consoling the sadness of an office worker" • *naishin "shimatta" to omoinagara* "while thinking to myself, 'I've gone and done it now'" • *ato ni wa hikezu [hikenai de]* "unable to stop now (lit., 'withdraw to the back'; i.e., retreat, start over)" • *utsumuite [utsumuku] yuku dansei-shain no kao o minagara [miru]* "while looking at the faces of the male employees, who had started to hang their heads" • *watashi wa utaitsuzukeru [utau + tsuzukeru] shika nakatta* "I had no choice but to continue singing" • *shiawase fu-shiawase mazete [mazeru] agerū [ageru]* "I mix happiness with unhappiness (for you)" • *konya wā [wa] yōkosō [yōkoso]* "welcome here tonight" • *koko wa Gokuraku-dōri* "this is Paradise Street" • *anna ni moriagatte [moriagaru] ita ba wa* "the scene (lit., 'place'), which had been so lively" • *ikki ni shizumari [shizumaru]* "in one stroke grew still" • *utaiowatta [utau + owaru] watashi wa* "I, who had finished singing" • *jigoku-dōri kara yatte kita fukitsu na onna ni natte ita* "I had become the unlucky

❖ *shimatta*: a mild curse when having done something stupid or been caught in an awkward situation (here Sakura realizes she has chosen an inappropriate song). ❖ *yōkoso*: lit., "quite good"; here, a set greeting of welcome, and may be followed by *irasshai[mase]*. ❖ *hari no mushiro o aruku*: a variation of the set expression *hari no mushiro ni suwaru* (sit on a bed of thorns).

woman (who had come) from Hell Street" • *hari no mushiro o aruku yō na omoi de* "feeling as though I were walking on a bed of thorns (lit., 'mat of needles')" • *seki ni modori [modoru]* "I went back to my seat" • *hikitsutta [hikitsuru] mama no kao de* "with a drawn look still on my face" • *bīru o gokuri to nomihoshita [nomihosu]* "I downed my beer in a gulp"

た。

昨日の失敗を今日に持ち越している余裕はない。

それがOLの人生である。

私は一生懸命パソコンのキーボードを叩き、注文書等の情報をインプットする作業に励んだ。

しかし、他の同期が五十できるところを私は三十しかできず、しかも間違いが多い。簡単な宛て名書きすら注意力散漫な私は書き損じてしまい、隣の貧相な男から何度も軽蔑（けいべつ）の眼差（まなざ）しを向けられていた。

実はこの頃、会社には内緒で漫画の仕事も兼ねていたので睡眠時間が足りず、仕事中に往々（おうおう）にして睡魔（すいま）が襲って来たのである。

ボーっとした頭に睡魔がしのび寄ると、夢か現（うつつ）か

- *kinō no shippai o kyō ni mochikoshite iru yoyū wa nai* "you can't afford the luxury of carrying (lit., 'don't have the leeway to carry') yesterday's mistakes over to today" • *sore ga ō-eru no jinsei de aru* "that's the life of an OL" • *watashi wa isshō-kenmei pasokon no kībōdo o tataki [tataku]* "I pounded away at the keyboard of my computer terminal for all I was worth" • *chūmon-sho nado no jōhō o inputto suru sagyō ni hagenda [hagemu]* "I applied myself to the task of inputting data like orders and such" • *shikashi* "however" • *hoka no dōki ga gojū dekiru tokoro o watashi wa sanjū shika dekizu [= dekinai de]* "I could only do 30 (orders) where my fellow newcomers could do 50" • *shikamo* "moreover" • *machigai ga ōi* "there were (i.e., I made) many mistakes" • *kantan na atenagaki sura* "even writing simple addresses" • *chūi-ryoku sanman na watashi wa* "I, who was easily distracted (lit., 'of scattered attention')" • *kakisonjite shimai [shimau]* "I miswrote (them)" • *tonari no hinsō na otoko kara* "from the seedy person next to me" • *nando mo keibetsu no manazashi o mukerarete [mukeru] ita* "I received scornful looks any number of times" • *jitsu wa* "actually" • *kono koro* "around that time" • *kaisha ni wa naisho de* "without the company knowing (lit., 'in secret from the company')" • *manga no shigoto mo kanete [kaneru] ita no de* "since I was at the same time working on *manga*" • *suimin-*

❖ *yoyū wa nai*: don't have the extra margin of time, money, mental energy, etc. to do something; cf. *yoyū ga aru*. ❖ *hoka no dōki*: i.e., *hoka no dōki no ō-eru–tachi*. ❖ *mukerarete ita*: *muku* = to point something in a certain direction; here in the so-called suffering passive. ❖ *kono koro*: note that *kono koro* (about that time) and *kono goro* (recently) can be written with the same *kanji*. ❖ *suima ga osotte kita*: (lit., "the sleep-demon attacked"); a set phrase.

---

jikan ga tarizu [tarinai de] "I wasn't getting enough sleep (lit., 'sleep-hours were lacking')" • *shigoto-chū ni ōō ni shite* "frequently while working" • *suima ga osotte [osou] kita no de aru* "I would get sleepy (lit., 'the sleep-demon attacked')" • *bōtto shita atama ni suima ga shinobiyoru to* "when the sleep-demon would creep up on my groggy head" • *yume ka utsutsu ka wakaranaku nari [naru]* "I couldn't tell whether it was a dream or reality"

わからなくなり、隣の貧相な男に「……だから山田さんは上手だったって言ったじゃないですか、あれはなかなか良かったですね」などと急にブツブツ喋りかけたりして、ハッと気がつくと貧相な男の驚愕にひきつった顔がアップで現れるというような事もしばしば起こっていた。

ある日、パソコンを打っていた私はまたも睡魔に襲われ、顔をゴンッとキーボードに叩きつけてしまった。

パソコンのモニターはビーーッとメチャクチャになり、私はハッと青ざめた。なんと、私のパソコンのモニターだけでなく、並んでいるパソコン全部が関連して ビーーッとなってしまったのだ。こんなにもパソコン同士は仲が良かったのか……。

• *tonari no hinsō na otoko ni* "to the seedy person next to me" • *... da kara Yamada-san wa jōzu da tte [da to] itta ja nai desu ka* "... that's why I said Yamada was good, didn't I" • *are wa nakanaka yokatta desu ne* "that was really good, wasn't it" • *nado* "etc. (i.e., the two clauses above are two examples of what she said to the seedy person)" • *to kyū ni butsubutsu shaberikaketari shite* "(... so saying,) I would suddenly start mumbling or something to him • *hatto ki ga tsuku to* "when I suddenly realized (what I was doing)" • *hinsō na otoko no kyōgaku ni hikitsutta [hikitsuru] kao ga appu de arawareru* "the seedy person's face drawn up in astonishment would appear in close-up" • *to iu yō na koto mo shiba-shiba okotte [okoru] ita* "such things frequently occurred" • *aru hi* "one day (lit., 'a certain day')" • *pasokon o utte [utsu] ita watashi wa* "working at (lit., 'hitting') my computer, I" • *mata mo* "once again" • *suima ni osoware [osou]* "I was attacked by the sleep-demon" • *kao o gontto kībōdo ni tatakitsukete shimatta* "I hit my head (lit., 'face') against the keyboard with a bang" • *pasokon no monitā wa bītto mechakucha ni nari [naru]* "the computer monitor beeped and went crazy" • *watashi wa hatto aozameta [aozameru]* "startled, I went white as a sheet" • *nanto* "lo and behold!" • *watashi no pasokon no monitā dake de naku* "it wasn't only my computer monitor" • *narande [narabu] iru pasokon zenbu ga*

❖ *butsubutsu shaberikaketari*: *butsubutsu iu* is also used. ❖ *appu de*: "up" as in a close-up shot in a movie. ❖ *pasokon*: contraction of *pasonaru konpyūtā*. ❖ *gontto*: sound of two heavy objects striking one another; also *gotsun*. ❖ *bīto [iu oto]*: used for high-pitched sounds made by beepers or the tone of an answering machine. ❖ *mechakucha*: broadly describes a state of disorder. ❖ *nanto*: used to introduce something startling. ❖ *naka ga yokatta*: of course, *naka ga ii* usually refers only to living creatures.

---

kanren shite [suru] "the lined-up computers acted in unison (lit., 'in conjunction')" • *bītto natte [naru] shimatta no da* "they beeped (and went on the blink)" • *konna ni mo pasakon dōshi wa naka ga yokatta [yoi] no ka ...* "you mean computers get along so well?"

私がぼんやりパソコン同士の仲の良さを感心していると、周りは大騒ぎになっていた。

班の係長は「君はただでさえも注意力が足りないのだから、気をひきしめて、居眠りなんかされては困る」というような事をクドクド言っていた。

私は心底すまないと思い「すみません」と頭を下げ、一分も経たないうちにまた睡魔と格闘していた。

こんな調子であったから、班の男性社員からは相当顰蹙をかっていた。それは当然の事である。しかし、違う班の人々からは意外と人気があり、色物担当の女としては上々の役割を果たしていた気がする。

四月も十日を過ぎた頃、『営業課花見大会』が催さ

• watashi ga bonyari pasokon-dōshi no naka no yosa o kanshin shite iru to "as I was blankly marveling at the compatibility of the computers" • mawari wa ōsawagi ni natte ita "around me a great uproar had broken out (lit., 'all around had become uproar')" • han no kakari-chō wa "the assistant section chief of my unit" • kimi wa "you (informal)" • tada de sae mo "even at the best of times" • chūi-ryoku ga tarinai no da kara "because you are lacking in the ability to concentrate (lit., 'because [in your case] the ability to concentrate is insufficient')" • ki o hikishimete [hikishimeru] "pull yourself together (lit., 'tighten your spirit')" • ine-muri nanka sarete wa komaru "we can't have you dozing off and things (lit., 'we will be troubled, your napping off and whatnot')" • to iu yō na koto o kudokudo itte ita "he went on at length in that way" • watashi wa shinsoko sumanai to omoi [omou] "thinking from the bottom of my heart that it was inexcusable" • "sumimasen" to atama o sage [sageru] "I bowed my head and said, 'I'm sorry'" • ippun mo tatanai uchi ni "before even a minute had passed" • mata suima to kakutō shite ita "I was again struggling with the sleep-demon" • konna chōshi de atta kara "because things were like this" • han no dansei-shain kara wa "from the male employees in my unit" • sōtō "quite a bit, considerable" • hinshuku o katte [kau] ita "I earned disapproval (lit., 'bought frowns') • sore wa

❖ *tada de sae*: lit., "even ordinarily"; a fixed expression meaning roughly "it's bad enough as it is without adding to it." ❖ *sarete wa komaru*: a commonly used pattern; lit., "if you do ~, we will be troubled by it." ❖ *hitobito kara wa ~ ninki ga ari*: ordinarily, the phrase would be *hitobito ni wa ~ ninki ga ari*; with the verb *yoserare [yoserareru* = to be gathered, gained, *kara* would be standard. The author seems to have combined two phrases in one. ❖ *hatashite ita ki ga suru*: verb / adjective + *ki ga suru* = feel that ~ . ❖ *hanami-taikai*: outdoor parties under the cherry trees are very common when the cherry blossoms are in full bloom.

tōzen no koto de aru "that was only natural" • *shikashi* "however" • *chigau han no hitobito kara wa* "with (lit., 'from') people in other units" • *igai to [to = ni] ninki ga ari* "I was surprisingly popular" • *iromono-tantō no onna toshite wa* "as the woman in charge of being entertaining" • *jōjō no yakuwari o hatashite [hatasu] ita ki ga suru* "I feel I did a pretty good job of performing the role (as)" • *shigatsu mo tōka o sugita koro* "in April, sometime around the tenth (lit., 'in April, sometime after the tenth had passed')" • *"eigyō-ka hanami-taikai" ga moyōsareru [moyōsu] koto ni natta* "it was decided that a Sales Section Cherry-Blossom Viewing Party would be held"

される事になった。あの新入社員歓迎会からまだ一週間も経っていないのに、またそんな事をするのか……と一抹の不安が過ぎった。またあの惨劇が……

私の胸はつまった。

せっかくの土曜日の午後をムダにするのは非常に辛かったのだが新人に選択の余地はない。ビールや酒を小高い丘の上まで運ばされ、上司が来る前に準備をしなくてはならないのだ。

続々と上司達がエビス顔で到着する。部長のあいさつが終わると、またも新人が芸を披露する番である。

歌を歌う者あり、踊りを踊る者あり、桜が乱れ散る中、ばかばかしい時間は大きなうねりとなって流れていった。

• *ano shinnyū-shain kangei-kai kara* "since the party for new employees" • *mada isshū-kan mo tatte [tatsu] inai no ni* "although not even one week had passed" • *mata sonna koto o suru no ka …* "they're going to do it again?" • *to ichimatsu no fuan ga yogitta* "a touch (lit., 'one brush-stroke') of uneasiness crossed (my mind)" • *mata ano sangeki ga* "once more that catastrophe (tragic event) …" • *watashi no mune wa tsumatta [tsumaru]* "I felt a weight on my chest (lit., 'my chest clogged up')" • *sekkaku no doyō-bi no gogo o muda ni suru no wa* "giving up (lit., 'wasting') a precious Saturday afternoon" • *hijō ni tsurakatta [tsurai] no da ga* "was very hard, but" • *shinjin ni sentaku no yochi wa nai* "newcomers don't have the luxury (lit., 'margin') of choice" • *bīru ya sake o kodakai oka no ue made hakobasare [hakobu]* "we had to carry (lit., 'were made to carry') the beer, *sake*, and other things to the top of a small hill" • *jōshi ga kuru mae ni* "before the higher-ups arrived" • *junbi o shinakute wa naranai no da* "we had to make the preparations" • *zokuzoku to* "one after the other" • *jōshi-tachi ga ebisu-gao de tōchaku suru* "the higher-ups arrived with beaming faces" • *buchō no aisatsu ga owaru to* "after opening remarks by the department head were finished" • *mata mo* "once again" • *shinjin ga gei o hirō suru ban de aru* "it was the turn of the newcomers to show off their talents" • *uta o utau mono ari [aru]* "there were

❖ *ano shinnyū-shain kangei-kai*: *ano* (or *are*) is used rather than *sono* (*sore*) to refer to things already talked about or known to both the speaker and listener. Cf. *ano sangeki* in the next sentence. ❖ *suru no ka*: *ka* here indicates a rhetorical question with implied criticism. ❖ *sekkaku*: often (but not always) indicates that it's a waste not to take advantage of some precious opportunity. ❖ *Ebisu-gao*: a set expression; Ebisu, one of the seven deities of good fortune, is traditionally portrayed with a jolly, laughing face. ❖ ~ *mono ari* ~ *mono ari*: literary parallel construction.

those who sang" • *odori o odoru mono ari* "there were those who danced" • *sakura ga midarechiru naka* "as (lit., 'in the midst of') cherry blossoms fell and scattered" • *bakabakashii jikan wa ōkina uneri to natte nagarete itta* "the ridiculous hours passed like a giant swell of waves"

何の芸もない男が、突然「セミになります」と絶叫したかと思うと、次の瞬間には木に飛びついて「ミーンミーン」と鳴き始めた。

恐怖のセミ男の登場に一同色めき立ち、「もっと上まで行け」のコールが飛び交い、引っ込みのつかなくなったセミ男はどんどん桜の木を登っていったのである。

桜の花びらがセミ男の顔にベタベタとつき、本物の怪人のようになりながら彼は鳴き続けた。私はその時、彼が一生ヒラで終わる予感を止める事ができなかった。

いよいよホコ先は私に向けられた。私は酔った勢いも手伝って、地元静岡の話題を落語風に語り始めた。「あれだね、静岡っつうとお茶が有名でね、も

• *nan no gei mo nai otoko ga* "some talentless man" • *totsuzen "semi ni narimasu" to zekkyō shita ka to omou to* "he suddenly shouted out, 'I will become a cicada,' and before you knew it he" • *tsugi no shunkan ni wa* "in the next instant" • *ki ni tobitsuite [tobitsuku]* "he attached himself (lit., 'jumped and clung') to a tree" • *"mīn mīn" to nakihajimeta* "he started imitating a cicada cry" • *kyōfu no semi-otoko no tōjō ni* "at the appearance of the terrible cicada-man" • *ichidō iromekitachi [iromekitatsu]* "everyone (lit., 'the assemblage') got excited" • *"motto ue made ike [iku]" no kōru ga tobikai [tobikau]* "calls were flying (here and there) of 'climb higher'" • *hikkomi no [=ga] tsukanaku natta semi-otoko wa* "having gone too far to stop now, the cicada-man • *dondon sakura no ki o nobotte itta no de aru* "he climbed further and further up the cherry tree" • *sakura no hanabira ga semi-otoko no kao ni betabeta to tsuki [tsuku]* "cherry petals stuck fast to the face of the cicada-man" • *honmono no kaijin no yō ni narinagara* "while becoming genuinely like some strange creature" • *kare wa nakitsuzuketa* "he continued making cicada sounds" • *sono toki* "then" • *kare ga isshō hira de owaru yokan o tomeru koto ga dekinakatta* "I couldn't help thinking (lit., 'couldn't stop the presentiment') that he would end his life at the bottom of the totem pole (i.e., would never be promoted to a managerial position)" • *iyoiyo*

❖ *nan no gei mo nai otoko*: literally, a man with no performing talents, but idiomatically a man who is devoid of any redeeming features: i.e., a hopeless case. ❖ *zekkyō shita ka to omou to*: *-ta ka to omou to* = *-ta totan [ni]* (just as ~ then ~); both are formulas and retain almost nothing of their original meanings ("think" in the first case and "road shoulder" in the second). ❖ *miin miin*: the sound made by cicadas. ❖ *nakihajimeta*: stem + *hajimeru* = to start to ~. ❖ *iromekitachi*: *iromeku* = lit., "to become colorful"; fig., suddenly to become nervous, lively, or excited (*tatsu* ["rise"] adds emphasis). ❖ *kōru*: perhaps from English "call." In this sense connotes a verbal demand or request (e.g., *kaere-kōru* = "come home call," a call to the office demanding that a working spouse come home early); a recent addition to the language among young people. ❖ *hikkomi ga tsukanai*: lit., "withdrawal doesn't stick"; *tsuku* (originally "to stick") has various meanings; here, to realize or bring to a conclusion a desired end; the set phrase = to be too late to back out. ❖ *betabeta [suru]*: used of things like sticky foods or wet clothes; also of a clinging or dependent person. ❖ *hira*: see note on *hira-shain* above where *hira* is written in *kanji*; *hira* is most likely written in *katakana* here because the single *kanji* would be hard to decipher at a glance. ❖ *rakugo-fū*: *rakugo* is a traditional form of comic storytelling; *fū* = in the style of. ❖ *are da ne*: in *rakugo* style but also in general conversation, a means of attracting people's attention, piquing their interest about the nature of *are*; also *are desu ne*.

"at last" • *hokosaki wa watashi ni mukerareta [mukeru]* "it was my turn (lit., 'the spear-tip was directed at me')" • *yoparatta ikioi mo tetsudatte [tetsudau]* "partly due to the fact that I was tipsy (lit., 'helped by the momentum of tipsiness')" • *jimoto Shizuoka no wadai o rakugo-fū ni katarihajimeta* "I started telling stories (lit., 'topics') about my home Shizuoka in *rakugo* style" • *are da ne* "well, let's see" • *Shizuoka ttsu to* (= *Shizuoka to iu to*) "as for Shizuoka" • *ocha ga yūmei de [de aru] ne* "it's famous for its tea"

ーどこ行っても茶畑ばっかりですわな、そりゃ。他の県との境界線ギリギリまで茶が植えてあるからね、遠くから見ても緑色に盛り上がってるとこが静岡県ってわかるくらいなもんで……」。もう、ある事ない事喋りまくり、酒のおかげで皆異常にウケていた。フト我に返ると、桜吹雪（さくらふぶき）の中で芸人になっている自分が人生を後ろ向きで歩んでいる事に気づき、空しかった。

五月下旬、またも居眠りをしている私を班の係長が呼び出し、「君はよく居眠りをしているが、何か夜の商売でもしているのかね」と、いやらしい目つきで詰問（きつもん）してきた。

私は内心ムッとしながら「はぁ、実は漫画を描いているものですから……」と気弱に答えると係長は

• *mō doko itte mo* "wherever you go there" • *chabatake bakkari [bakari] desu wa na, sorya [sore wa]* "there's nothing but tea fields in Shizuoka, that's for sure" • *hoka no ken to no kyōkai-sen girigiri made* "right up to the borderline with other prefectures" • *cha ga uete aru kara ne* "since tea plants are planted there, I'm telling you" • *tōku kara mite mo* "even if seen from a distance" • *midori-iro ni moriagatte 'ru toko [tokoro] ga Shizuoka-ken tte [de aru to] wakaru kurai na mon [mono] de [de aru]* … "just from the mounds of green you can tell that it's Shizuoka Prefecture (lit., 'you can understand it is Shizuoka Prefecture just from the fact that the place is rising up in green')" • *mō aru koto nai koto shaberimakuri [shaberimakuru]* "I talked a real blue streak, stretching the truth a bit (lit., 'talked on about things that are and aren't')" • *sake no okage de* "thanks to the liquor (everyone had drunk)" • *mina ijō ni ukete ita* "it was peculiarly well received by everyone" • *futo ware ni kaeru to* "when I suddenly returned to myself" • *sakura-fubuki no naka de geinin ni natte iru jibun ga* "having turned into an entertainer in the midst of the swirling cherry petals (lit., 'cherry snowstorm'), I myself" • *jinsei o ushiromuki de ayunde [ayumu] iru koto ni kizuki [kizuku]* "noticed that I was turning my back on life (lit., 'walking through life backwards')" • *munashikatta* "I felt empty inside (lit., 'was empty; meaningless')" •

❖ *mō doko itte*: *mō* here is a special usage, indicating that the following statement is without a doubt true; the dash is to emphasize the sound, the fact that this is the spoken word, not the written. ❖ *bakkari (bakari)*: the consonant is doubled for emphasis. ❖ *sorya*: partly used here, in the *rakugo* style, to maintain the rhythm and partly for emphasis. ❖ *girigiri*: commonly indicates an outermost limit or doing something at the last possible moment. ❖ *wakaru kurai*: lit., "to the extent that one can tell that ~ ." ❖ *mon de*: *mon* (*mono*) here indicates the speaker is making an objective statement about a state of affairs; *de* ... is a typical mid-sentence ending in *rakugo* style. ❖ *mō, aru koto*: see note above on *mō doko itte*. ❖ *jinsei o ushiromuki de*: a variation on the set phrase *jinsei ni se o mukeru* ("to turn one's back on life"). ❖ *gogatsu gejun*: months are divided into three parts: the *jōjun* (上旬) or first ten days, the *chūjun* (中旬) or middle ten days, and the *gejun* (下旬) or last ten days. ❖ *yoru no shōbai*: the usual phrase for work as a hostess in a bar or night club; *yoru no shigoto* would have no such connotations. ❖ *shite iru no ka ne*: *ka ne* indicates that the speaker has doubts and wishes to confirm those doubts. ❖ *haa*: acknowledges a question rather than giving a positive answer. ❖ *mono desu kara*: see note on *mon de* above.

---

gogatsu gejun "late in May" • *mata mo inemuri o shite iru watashi o* "I, who was nodding off once again" • *han no kakari-chō ga [watashi o] yobidashi [yobidasu]* "I was called before the assistant section chief of my unit (lit., 'the assistant section chief of my unit called me [who had nodded off once again] before him')" • *kimi wa yoku inemuri o shite iru ga* "you doze off quite a bit, and" • *nani ka yoru no shōbai de mo shite iru no ka ne* "could it be that you're doing some kind of night work?" • *to [itte], iyarashii metsuki de kitsumon shite kita* "(so saying,) he grilled me with a leer (lit., 'with a lascivious look in his eyes')" • *watashi wa naishin mutto shinagara* "while inwardly furious" • *"haa, jitsu wa manga o kaite iru mono desu kara ..." to* "(saying,) well, yes, actually it is because I am drawing comics" • *kiyowa ni kotaeru to* "when I timidly told him that ~ "

「そんなもん、会社か漫画かどっちかにしろ」と言ったので、私はすかさず「そりゃ、漫画にします」と答えた。

こうして私の辞職はあっさり決まった。課長は「いやぁ、君は面白いから会社を辞めるのは残念だが仕方ないねェ」と最後まで色物担当の私に未練を残してくれた。

この二カ月で私がやった事といえば、歓迎会で場をシラけさし、桜吹雪の中で漫談をし、パソコンを壊し、宛て名書きを間違え、封筒をムダにし、花見帰りのまんじゅうだけは、上司の分までもらって帰ったという呆れた事実だけである。

数日後、もちこされた四月分との二カ月分の給料が届いた。営業課の私の役割は、芸人としての営業

• *kakari-chō wa ~ to itta no de* "since the assistant section chief said, ' ~ ,'" • *sonna mon [=mono]* "is *that* all (lit., 'that kind of thing')" • *kaisha ka manga ka dotchi [dochira] ka ni shiro [suru]* "take one or the other—the company or comics" • *watashi wa sukasazu "sorya [sore wa], manga ni shimasu" to kotaeta* "I answered at once, 'then (lit., 'as for that') I'll take comics'" • *kōshite* "in this way" • *watashi no jishoku wa assari kimatta* "my resignation was decided without further ado (lit., 'simply')" • *iyā* "gee" • *kimi wa omoshiroi kara* "since you're so interesting" • *kaisha o yameru no wa zannen da ga* "it's a shame you're quitting the company, but" • *shikata ga nai nē" to [itte]* "(saying,) 'it can't be helped, can it'" • *saigo made* "to the (bitter) end" • *iromono-tantō no watashi ni miren o nokoshite kureta* "he was kind enough (= *kureru*) to retain some regret for me as the person in charge of being entertaining" • *kono nikagetsu de watashi ga yatta shigoto to ieba ~ to iu akireta jijitsu dake de aru* "as for what I did during these two months it was nothing but appalling things (lit., 'facts; truth') like ~" • *kangei-kai de ba o shirakesashi [shirakeru]* "I cast a wet blanket over the welcoming party" • *sakura-fubuki no naka de mandan o shi [suru]* "I did a 'comic talk' under the falling cherry blossoms (lit., 'in the midst of the cherry snow-storm')" • *pasokon o kowashi [kowasu]* "I broke the computers" • *atena-*

❖ *iyaa*: an exclamation indicating surprise etc. used mainly by men; the section chief in this case may not be all that surprised, however. ❖ *shikata (ga) nai*: a very common phrase to fatalistically accept some state of affairs, indicate that one is helpless or the situation hopeless, or that someone is beyond hope; informally *shō ga nai* (from *shiyō ga nai*). ❖ ~ *to ieba*: lit., "if you say"; a set phrase for singling out a topic. ❖ *shirake-sashi*: *shirakesasu* from *shirakeru* (lit., "to turn white"); i.e., to get bored, take the fun out of something. ❖ *manjū*: a kind of confectionary resembling a filled cookie. ❖ *akireta jijitsu*: *akireru* shows that one is amazed in a negative way at something; *akireta* alone is often used as an exclamation of mild disgust.

---

gaki o machigae [machigaeru] "I made mistakes in writing out addresses" • *fūtō o muda ni shi [suru]* "I wasted envelopes" • *hanami-gaeri no manjū dake wa, jōshi no bun made moratte [morau] kaetta* "I went so far as to take the souvenir *manjū* of the higher-ups (as well as my own) on the way back from the cherry-blossom viewing party" • *sūjitsu-go* "a few days later" • *mochikosareta [mochikosu] shigatsu-bun to no nikagetsu-bun no kyūryō ga todoita [todoku]* "two months' (worth of) salary, including that carried over from April, arrived" • *eigyō-ka no watashi no yakuwari wa* "my role in the sales section" • *geinin toshite no eigyō ni owatta [owaru]* "ended with (i.e., never went beyond) my duties as an entertainer"

に終わった。政府刊行物を出版しているあの会社は、三流芸人を二ヵ月も雇って社内を潤（うるお）していただけにすぎなかったのだ。

中島みゆき作詞「極楽通りへいらっしゃい」
日本音楽著作権協会（出）許諾番号第九〇五二一三〇一〇〇一号

• *seifu-kankō-butsu o shuppan shite iru ano kaisha wa* "that company, which publishes government publications" • *sanryū-geinin o nikagetsu mo yatotte [yatou]* "hired a third-rate entertainer for two months" • *shanai o uruoshite [uruosu] ita dake ni suginakatta no da* "it was nothing more than brightening up (lit., 'moistening; enriching') the workplace a little by ~ "

❖ *uruoshite ita dake ni suginakatta no da*: noun/verb + *ni suginai* = to be nothing more than ~ ; to be merely ~ .

Itō Seikō

Itō Seikō, born in Tokyo in 1961, is active as a comedian, television personality, and rap musician as well as a writer. After graduating from Waseda University he worked for a few years at the large publishing company Kodansha Ltd., among other things as an editor at *Hot Dog Press*, a magazine aimed at younger male readers. His first novel, the 1988 *No Life King*, was about children absorbed in video games; it was later made into a film by Ichikawa Jun. He is the author of a number of unusual books, such as *Sekai no popusu*, which combines commentary on world events with pop song lyrics.

His powerful essay here on the Tiananmen Incident and the Japanese response was originally published in an anthology dealing with that event.

First published in the JICC Booklet *Ten'anmon no hanshin*. Copyright 1989 by Itō Seikō. The essay appears in the author's book *Zenbun keisai*. Reprinted by permission of Shinchōsha and the author.

天安門事件のこと

いとうせいこう

私はあからさまな嘘が嫌いだ。
バレている嘘を平気でつき続ける奴が、たまらな
く嫌いだ。

非核三原則のことをいっているのではない。今は
天安門事件のことだ。

プロレスでいえば、凶器に気づいていながら見て
見ぬふりをするレフェリー。それが中国政府のスポ
ークスマンだった。しかもこれは、リングの上での
約束事ではないのである。あまりの厚顔無恥な嘘は、
私をほとんど半狂乱にしたといっていい。

私は外からの目、あるいは外への目を拒絶する者

- *Ten'anmon jiken no koto* "about the Tiananmen Incident" • *watashi wa akarasama na uso ga kirai da* "I hate out-and-out lies" • *barete (bareru) iru uso o* "lies that have been exposed (for what they are)" • *heiki de tsukitsuzukeru [tsuku + tsuzukeru] yatsu ga* "those who unashamedly (lit., 'placidly') continue telling" • *tamaranaku kirai da* "I can't stand them" • *hikaku sangensoku no koto o itte (iu) iru no de wa nai* "I'm not talking here about the three non-nuclear principles" • *ima wa Ten'anmon jiken no koto da* "here I mean (lit., 'now it is') the Tiananmen Incident" • *puroresu de ieba* "put in terms of professional wrestling" • *kyōki ni kizuite (kizuku) inagara* "while being aware of dangerous weapons (being used in the ring)" • *mite (miru) minu (=minai) furi o suru refuerī* "(it's like) referees who pretend not to see them" • *sore ga Chūgoku seifu no supōkusuman datta* "that (i.e., being like a referee) was the Chinese government spokesmen (i.e., what the spokesman did)" • *shikamo* "moreover" • *kore wa ringu no ue de no yakusoku-goto de wa nai no de aru* "this is not a convention of the ring (i.e., this is not part of the agreed-upon rules that apply in the ring)" • *amari no kōgan-muchi na uso wa* "such bare-faced lies" • *watashi o hotondo han-kyōran ni shita to itte (iu) ii* "it is no exaggeration to say they drove me almost half-crazy" • *soto kara no me* "outside eyes (i.e., people looking in from the out-

❖ *Ten'anmon jiken no koto*: the killing of students at Tiananmen Square by the Chinese army in June of 1989; *koto* here, in a dictionary definition, refers to circumstances about, and limited to, the modifying word preceding it (cf. *hikaku sangensoku no koto* below and *Ten'anmon no koto* below). ❖ *uso o heiki de tsuki*: the phrase is *uso o tsuku* (to tell lies); *uso o iu* is also possible. ❖ *yatsu*: in reference to people, generally derogatory. ❖ *tamaranaku kirai*: *tamaranai* = unbearable, insufferable; cf. *okashikute tamaranai, tamaranakute okashī*, be unbearably funny. ❖ *hikaku sangensoku*: the policy that Japan will not produce, possess, or have on its soil nuclear weapons. ❖ *puroresu*: contraction of *purofesshonaru resuringu* (professional wrestling); matches in Japan are generally recognized as being rigged, with hidden razor blades and the like used to cause dramatic bleeding. ❖ *(puro resu) de ieba*: (lit., "if said of ~ ") a common pattern for making an analogy; the literal meaning of *iu* has faded almost to non-existence. ❖ *mite minu (=minai) furi o suru*: = idiomatic for "pretend not to see, turn a blind eye to"; *~furi o suru* = "pretend to ~" ❖ *suru referī*: the missing verb might be something like *ga sore (=yatsu) da* ("the referee is like those liars"), referring back to *uso o heiki de tsuki-tsuzukeru yatsu*. ❖ *hotondo han-kyōran*: the duplication in meaning of *hotondo* and *han-* ("almost half-crazy") is typical of the spoken language. ❖ *yakusokugoto*: lit., "promised thing"; here something implicitly agreed upon by all parties. ❖ *kōgan-muchi na (no)*: set phrase = "shameless, brazen"; lit., "thick-faced and shameless." ❖ *~ to itte ii*: lit., "it is all right to say that …"; a common pattern, slightly more direct than *to itte mo ii*.

side)" • *aruiwa soto e no me o* "or eyes directed outside"

が嫌いなのだ。内側さえごまかしておけば何とかなる、と思う奴が憎たらしくて仕方ないのである。

その意味において、中国の学生たちはひたすら外を向いていた。メディアを通して国外へメッセージを伝える戦略は、何と開放的だったことだろう。あの戦い方がメディアにおける一大革命だったことに間違いはない。

事件後、密告電話をパンクさせるために中国へコールを続ける人々がいた。いわばメディア・テロだ。天安門での闘争が、まさにメディアに関わる事柄であったことを、彼ら電話ハッカーたちは十分に知っていたのだと思う。

メディアは外を向く。外に向けてメッセージを開く。

• *kyozetsu suru mono ga kirai na no da* "I hate those who reject (such eyes)" • *uchigawa sae* "even if only (those on) the inside (i.e., within the group, nation, `etc.)" • *gomakashite (gomakasu) okeba (oku) nan to ka naru to omou yatsu ga* "those who think things will turn out all right if they deceive them (i.e., jokers who think that things will work themselves out if they hoodwink (those on the inside)" • *nikutarashikute shikata nai no de aru* "they are just too terrible for words" • *sono imi ni oite* "in that sense" • *Chūgoku no gakusei-tachi wa* "the Chinese students" • *hitasura soto o muite (muku) ita* "were steadfastly looking outward" • *media o tōshite* "via the (mass) media" • *kokugai e messēji o tsutaeru senryaku wa* "the strategy of sending their message outside the country" • *nan to kaihō-teki datta koto darō* "what a liberated (i.e., emancipated, open and aboveboard) thing that was to do!" • *ano tatakai-kata ga media ni okeru ichidai-kakumei datta* "that way of fighting (i.e., tactics) was a great revolution in (the use of) the media" • *koto ni machi-gai wa nai* "there is no doubt (lit., 'no mistake') that ~ " • *jiken-go* "after the (Tiananmen) Incident" • *mikkoku denwa o panku saseru tame ni* "in order to overoad the telephone (lines), (carrying calls) informing (against the students)" • *Chūgoku e kōru o tsuzukeru hitobito ga ita* "there were people who continued to call China (i.e., repeatedly called Chinese tele-

❖ *gomakashite okeba*: note the use of the helping verb *oku* for something done in preparation for the future. ❖ *nan to ka naru*: idiom = "somehow it will turn out all right; somehow we will manage." ❖ *nikutarashikute shikata nai*: idiomatic use of *shikata (ga) nai*: to be so hateful one cannot stand it (see also *abunakkashikute shikata ga nai* below). ❖ *nan to kaihō-teki datta koto darō*: *nan to ~ darō* = what a ~ !; how ~ ! ❖ *tatakaikata*: stem + *kata* = way of -ing. ❖ *ni okeru*: indicates the place or time at which something took place. ❖ *ichidai*: prefixed to nouns, means "big" or "important." ❖ *machigai wa nai*: idiomatic; "it is none other than ~ ; you may be sure that ~ ." ❖ *panku saseru*: *panku* derives from "puncture" (= blowout of a tire) and by extension means the overloading and failure of a telephone system etc.

phone numbers)" • *iwaba* "so to speak; in a manner of speaking" • *media-tero da* "it was media terrorism" • *Ten'anmon de no tōsō ga masa ni media ni kakawaru kotogara de atta koto o* "the fact that the conflict (struggle) at Tiananmen was truly an affair concerning the media" • *karera denwa hakkā-tachi wa jūbun ni shitte (shiru) ita no da to omou* "I think that they, the telephone hackers, were fully aware of ~ • *media wa soto o muku* "the media faces outwards" • *soto ni mukete (mukeru) messēji o hiraku* "it sends (lit., 'opens') messages directed to the outside"

そして、そのメディアと連結してしまった以上、我々は態度を決定しなければならない。例えば「戦車の前に立った男」について、我々は態度決定を迫られる。魂を揺さぶられるか、バカじゃねえのかと思うかは勝手だが、ともかくそのことをどう受け止めるのかを決定すべきなのだ。

なぜなら、彼は戦車の前に立つと同時に、カメラの前にも立っていたからである。いわば、彼は我々に一人々々のモニターの前にも立っていたのだ。メディアを通して、彼は私の、そしてあなたの至近距離にいたのである。これはあくまで事実なのだ。

ところが、こうして距離を越えて外に向かった映像に対して、日本人の大半はどんな態度決定もしなかった。何が〝高度情報化社会〟だというのだろう

• *soshite* "and" • *sono media to renketsu shite shimatta ijō* "once we are hooked into that media" • *wareware wa taido o kettei shinakereba naranai* "we must determine our attitude (i.e., stance)" • *tatoeba* "for example" • *"sensha no mae ni tatta (tatsu) otoko" ni tsuite* "concerning 'the man who stood in front of the tank'" • *wareware wa taido-kettei o semarareru (semaru)* "we are pressed to determine our position" • *tamashii o yusaburareru (yusaburu) ka* "whether one's soul is stirred or" • *baka ja nē* [vulgar for *nai*] *no ka to omou ka wa* "or whether one thinks he's just dead from the neck up" • *katte da ga* "is up to you" • *tomokaku* "at any rate" • *sono koto o dō uketomeru no ka o kettei subeki na no da* "one has to (lit., 'should') decide how one reacts to that" • *naze nara ~ kara de aru* "the reason is ~ " • *kare wa sensha no mae ni tatsu to dōji ni* "at the same time that he was standing in front of the tank" • *kamera no mae ni mo tatte ita* "he was also standing in front of the cameras" • *iwaba* "so to speak; in a manner of speaking" • *kare wa wareware ni hitori-hitori no monitā no mae ni mo tatte ita no da* "he was also standing in front of us, each a monitor" • *media o tōshite* "by means of the media" • *kare wa watashi no, soshite anata no shikin-kyori ni ita no de aru* "he was at point-blank range for me and for you" • *kore wa akumade* _jijitsu_ *na no da* "that is the out-and-out truth (lit., 'this is absolutely the

❖ *renketsu shite shimatta ijō*: ~*ta* + *ijō* = after -ing, having -ed; implies that an action must be continued once started or that the consequences of an action must be accepted. ❖ *sensha no mae ni tatta otoko*: i. e., the famous news film of a Chinese man stopping a column of tanks by standing in front of the first one. ❖ *katte da ga*: *katte* often connotes a selfish or abitrary choice; *Katte ni shiro!* = "Please yourself; Do what you want (but don't blame me when it backfires)." ❖ *uketomeru*: in origin, means to be on the receiving end of some action and by extension, to be conscious of, or react internally to, a stimulus from the outside; can be translated in this sense as "respond to, react to, handle, deal with (all in a psychological sense)." ❖ *naze nara*: lit., "if (one were to ask) why"; a common transition. ❖ *hitori-hitori*: the ヽ mark is a ditto mark; usage varies, but here two marks mean that both *kanji* are repeated. ❖ *akumade*: *aku* = *akiru* (to be tired of); lit., "to the extent that one is tired of it" (i.e., absolutely); *akumade mo* is also common. ❖ *jijitsu*: the marks (called *bōten*) next to the *kanji* act as accent marks similar to italics or underlining in English.

---

truth')" • *tokoroga* "however; nonetheless" • *kōshite kyori o koete (koeru) soto ni mukatta (mukau) eizō ni taishite* "toward (these) images directed to the outside (world) from a great distance (lit., 'and overcoming distance') in this way" • *Nihon-jin no taihan wa* "the majority of Japanese" • *donna taido-kettei mo shinakatta* "made no determination of stance whatsoever" • *nani ga "kōdo-jōhōka shakai" da to iu no darō ka* "So much for the (Japan's) vaunted (lit., 'what is it they call Japan's') 'advanced information society'!"

か。日本人はまるで神のような気分で、"遠い国"の出来事を上からのぞき込んでいただけなのだ。とんでもない尊大さである。

私は別に「アメリカやフランスのような意思表示をしろ」というわけではない。彼らはそもそもああいうことに一致団結して憤慨するのが好きなのだ。むしろ、一致団結の憤慨に、私は賛成しない（たかがウサギを殺したぐらいのことでヒステリックになるような国民では危なっかしくて仕方がないからだ）。ただ、アメリカやフランスの人々には外からの目に対する意識があることを評価したいのである。かっこつけちゃったりする嫌らしさが鼻につくけれど、日本のように外からの目をまるで意識しないよりはよほどマシではないか。

• *Nihon-jin wa* "Japanese" • *marude kami no yō na kibun de* "acting (lit., 'with the feeling') as if they were gods" • *"tōi kuni" no dekigoto o ue kara nozokikonde (nozokikomu) ita dake na no da* "they did nothing but look down from above on the happenings in a 'faraway land'" • *tonde mo nai sondaisa de aru* "that's unspeakable arrogance" • *watashi wa betsu ni ~ to iu wake de wa nai* "it is not that I'm particularly saying (I don't especially mean) ~ " • *"America ya Furansu no yō na ishi-hyōji o shiro"* "take an adamant stance like America or France (lit., 'Express your will like America or France')" • *karera wa* "they (i.e., Americans, French, etc.)" • *somosomo* "in the first place; from the beginning" • *ā iu koto ni itchi-danketsu shite fungai suru no ga suki na no da* "they like uniting together in (righteous) indignation over such things" • *mushiro* "rather; if anything" • *itchi-danketsu no fungai ni watashi wa sansei shinai* "I don't approve of (lit., 'agree with') group indignation" • *takaga usagi o koroshita gurai no koto de* "about something as trivial as killing a rabbit" • *histerikku ni naru yō na kokumin de wa* "with a people who get hysterical about" • *abunakkashikute (abunakkashii = abunai) shikata ga nai kara da* "because it's enough to make one break out in a cold sweat (lit., 'because it's just too risky')" • *tada ~ hyōka shitai no de aru* "still, I want to recognize (lit., 'rate positively') that ~ " • *America ya*

❖ *nani ga* ~ : a form of rhetorical question which is usually followed by an answer: *Nani ga kokusai-ka. Chittomo kawatte inai ja nai ka* "What's all this talk of internationalization? Things haven't changed a bit". ❖ *marude kami no yō na*: here *marude* = "exactly like ~ ; as if ~ ." ❖ *tonde mo nai*: set phrase for something ridiculous or unthinkable; often used as an exclamation. ❖ *betsu ni*: *betsu ni* ~ *de wa nai* = not particularly, not especially. ❖ *to iu wake de wa nai*: *wake* here has a nominalizing function and can be replaced by *koto*. ❖ *takaga*: "only, merely," modifying *usagi o koroshita*. ❖ *usagi o koroshita*: apparently refers to protests against testing new drugs on animals. ❖ *shikata ga nai kara da*: *kara* is giving the reason for the preceding *sansei shinai*. ❖ *hyōka shitai*: *hyōka suru* = "evaluate" or, as here, "evaluate favorably." ❖ *kakko tsukechattari suru*: the use of ~*tari suru* adds the meaning of "do such things as"; -*chattari* is a contraction of -*te shimattari*; *kakko* (= *kakkō*) *o tsukeru* = to do something for the sake of appearance; to grandstand. ❖ *hana ni tsuku*: similar to the English "stick in one's craw."

Furansu no hitobito ni wa soto kara no me ni taisuru ishiki ga aru koto o "the people of America or France are conscious of the eyes of the outside (world) upon them" • *kakko (kakkō) tsukechattari (tsukete shimattari) suru iyarashisa ga hana ni tsuku keredo* "although I get tired of their disgusting posturing and whatnot (lit., 'the disagreeableness of their posturing and whatnot sticks in the nose [i.e., raises a stench]')" • *Nihon no yō ni* "like Japan" • *soto kara no me o marude ishiki shinai yori wa yohodo mashi de wa nai ka* "isn't it much better than not being conscious of the eyes of the outside (world) at all?"

この　"外からの目"のなさが、さっき書いた
"神のような気分"の原因であることは明らかだ。
ただどこからともなく世界をながめる視点。そして、
その自分が見られていないと思い込むこと。日本人
は情報社会の先端にいて、神のような鎖国をしてい
るのである。

外を知らずにいた鎖国は遠い昔のこと。いまや
我々は外のすべてを知りながら、なおかつ鎖国する。
徹底的な開国に見せかけた鎖国。

こいつは実にやっかいだ。

中国政府の鎖国姿勢と、この日本の鎖国姿勢はほ
とんど対をなしている。ただ、鎖国する主体がどこ
にあるかが異なるだけなのだ。一方は高圧的な政府、
そして一方は　"世間"という名のわかりにくいム

• kono "soto kara no me" no nasa (nai) ga ~ no gen'in de aru "this absence of 'eyes (looking) from the outside' is the cause of ~ " •sakki kaita (kaku) "kami no yō na kibun" "the 'God-like feeling' I wrote about earlier" • koto wa akiraka da "it is clear that ~" • tada doko kara to mo naku sekai o nagameru shiten "the perspective of merely gazing at the world from nowhere (in particular)" • soshite "and" • sono jibun ga mirarete inai to omoikomu koto "being under the impression that no one (outside) is looking at one (while one is looking outward)" • jōhō-shakai no sentan ni ite (iru) "while being in the vanguard of information societies" • kami no yō na sakoku o shite iru no de aru "are making a god-like (i.e., looking down from above) isolated country (i.e., are isolating themselves in a god-like manner)" • soto o shirazu (shiranaide) ni ita sakoku wa tōi mukashi no koto "(Japan) being an isolated country knowing nothing of the outside (world) is a thing of the long-ago (lit., 'far-away') past" • imaya "right now" • wareware wa "we (collective) • soto no subete o shirinagara "while knowing everything about the outside (world)" • naokatsu sakoku suru "and yet we isolate the country" • tettei-teki na kaikoku ni misekaketa sakoku "(it's) an isolated country in the guise of a completely open country" • koitsu wa jitsu ni yakkai da: "this is really a hard one" • Chūgoku seifu no sakoku shisei to "the isolated posture of the Chinese

❖ *mashi*: always has a negative nuance: the lesser of two evils. ❖ *nagameru shiten*: this incomplete sentence, and the one that follows, are supplying instances of the argument in the preceding sentence; both in outline form. ❖ *omoikomu*: connotes a belief (i.e., thinking something) without sufficient (or with mistaken) evidence. ❖ *sakoku*: historical term used for the "closed country" policy followed by the shogunate from the beginning of the 17th century to the "opening" of Japan by Perry in 1853. ❖ *shirazu*: = *shiranaide*; ~*zu* is a negative form from classical Japanese. ❖ *shirinagara*: stem + *nagara* = while ~ing. ❖ *naokatsu*: "and yet" (lit., "still" + "at the same time"). ❖ *misekaketa*: *misekakeru* = to make out to be, feign to be. ❖ *koitsu*: = "this guy" or "this one" with derogatory or sometimes affectionate connotations, with related forms *aitsu* and *soitsu*; can also mean "this thing or event." ❖ *yakkai*: refers to something that is troublesome or awkward.❖ *tsui o nashite*: *tsui* = a pair, a set; *nasu* = to form. ❖ *ippō wa ~ ippō wa*: on the one hand [is] ~ on the other [is] ~ .

---

government and" • *kono Nihon no sakoku shisei wa* "this isolated posture of Japan" • *~ to ~ wa hotondo tsui o nashite (nasu) iru* "~ and ~ almost form equivalents" • *tada* "it is just that" • *sakoku suru shutai ga doko ni aru ka ga kotonaru dake na no da* "they differ only in where the core of isolationism is (located)" • *ippō wa kōatsu-teki na seifu* "on the one hand is an oppressive government" • *soshite* "and" • *ippō wa "seken" to iu na no wakarinikui mūdo* "on the other) is an elusive (lit., 'difficult to grasp') mood going under the name of 'public opinion'"

ード。つまり、我々日本人は自分で自分を鎖国している。罪も罰もないがゆえに決して破ることのできない掟。その中に、我々は生かされているのだ。

話が若干それた。申し訳ない。だが、中国で起きたことはこのように他人事ではない。それは、外へ向い外から来る情報を押えつけられ、生き生きとした交通を断たれた者の戦いなのだから。その戦いに勝利する方法は、ただひたすら交通しあうことに違いない。互いにメディアを連結させ、どのようにそれを断たれようとも、あらゆるやり方でまた結び合う。どんなメッセージを運ぼうとかまわない。とにかくメディアの網の目をこの世界に張りめぐらせることなのだ。

• *tsumari* "in other words" • *wareware Nihon-jin wa* "we Japanese" • *jibun de jibun o sakoku shite iru* "we ourselves are isolating ourselves" • *tsumi mo batsu mo nai ga yue ni* "as a result of the fact that there is no crime and punishment (i.e., involved in the question under discussion)" • *kesshite yaburu koto no dekinai okite* "(there are) mores (lit., 'rules') which must never be broken" • *sono naka ni wareware wa ikasarete (ikasu) iru no da* "we are living (lit., 'allowed to live') under those conditions (lit., 'in the midst [of those conditions]')" • *hanashi ga jakkan soreta (soreru)* "the discussion has gotten somewhat off track" • *mōshiwake nai*: "I apologize" • *da ga* "but yet" • *Chūgoku de okita koto wa* "what happened in China" • *kono yō ni* "in this way" • *taningoto de wa nai* "is not entirely irrelevant (lit., 'is not someone else's matter')" • *wareware no mondai de mo aru no da* "it is also our problem as well" • *sore wa ~ na no da kara* "that is because ~ " • *soto e mukai soto kara kuru jōhō o osaetsukerare (osaetsukeru)* "information going to the outside, (and information) coming in from the outside, has been suppressed" • *iki-iki to shita kōtsū o tatareta (tatsu) mono no tatakai na no da kara* "(because it's) a battle by people whose lively communications (lit., 'traffic') have been severed" • *sono tatakai ni shōri suru hōhō wa* "the way to achieve victory in that battle" • *tada hitasura kōtsū shiau*

❖ *seken*: = the world, life, people (in the world), society, here referring to peer pressure, what "they" will say. ❖ *nai ga yue ni*: *yue* = reason, cause (but also lineage, a history); a literary word with many complications, it follows nouns and verbs with the meaning here: "for that reason, consequently, accordingly". The *ga* following *nai* is idiomatic usage. *Nai ga yue ni* is more literary than *nai kara* as *aru ga yue ni* is than *aru kara*. ❖ *okite*. ❖ *de mo aru*: note that the set *de aru* is broken by *mo* ("also"). ❖ *taningoto*: *tanin* (lit., "other people") are those outside a particular group based on family, school, work, etc.; *taningoto* might be translated as "other people's business" (synonymous with *hitogoto*). ❖ *(shiau koto) ni chigai nai*: lit. "there is no mistake that it is ~ ; it is none other than to ~ ; is no doubt but to ~ ." ❖ *dono yō ni sore o tatareyō tomo*: *dono yō ni ~ -yō/ō tomo* = no matter how ~ (= *dono yō ni ~ -te mo*). ❖ *donna messēji o hakobō to*: *donna ~ ~yō/ō to* = no matter what ~ . ❖ *kamawanai*: (*kamau*) in the negative indicates that one doesn't care or mind about something, often about which choice is made; *okamai naku* is a polite phrase used by guests, protesting that the host should not go to any trouble in terms of preparing food etc. ❖ *harimeguraseru*: the difference between *harimegurasu* (to spread) and *harimeguraseru* (to have spread) is that the former indicates the action itself whereas the latter indicates the completion of the action. *-Seru* can be appended to certain other verbs with a similar meaning.

---

koto ni chigai nai "there is no doubt that it is quite simply to communicate (lit., 'to traffic')" • *tagai ni media o renketsu sase (saseru)* "(we) mutually link up our media" • *dono yō ni sore o tatareyō (tatsu) tomo* "and no matter how (others) may try to sever them" • *arayuru yarikata de mata musubiau* "(we) must reconnect them by every means possible" • *donna messēji o hakobō (hakobu) to kamawanai* "it doesn't matter what sorts of messages are carried" • *tonikaku* "at any rate" • *media no ami no me o kono sekai ni harimeguraseru (harimegurasu)* "to have spread the media net (lit., 'the meshes of a net') over the world" • *koto na no da* "the (important) thing is ~ "

閉じようとする者、鎖国を好む者にとって、その運動こそが脅威となるだろう。中国人民のいう "対話" とは、そのような運動のことだったのだと思う。メッセージが互いに異なろうと、とにかく話し合うこと。その話し合う場、それ自体がメディアなのだから。

こうして中国人民の一人々々が作ったメディアを、私が断ってはならないと思う。発言であれ、態度決定であれ、行動であれ、ともかく何か反応をしなければ、そこでメディアを閉じることになってしまう。私もあなたも、もしメディアを断ち切りたくなかったら、あの天安門から発信された何かに反応し続けるべきだ。もし、鎖国にいら立っているなら、メディアをつなぎ合わせて世界を開放すべきなの

• *tojiyō (tojiru) to suru mono [ni totte]* "(for) those who are trying to close (the doors)" • *sakoku o konomu mono ni totte* "for those who prefer an isolated country" • *sono undō koso ga kyōi to naru darō* "they will probably find just such a movement threatening (lit., 'that movement itself will become a threat')" • *Chūgoku jinmin no iu "taiwa" to wa* "what Chinese citizens were calling 'dialogue'" • *sono yō na undō no koto datta no da to omou* "I think it was (precisely) that sort of movement" • *messēji ga tagai ni kotonarō (kotonaru) to* "even if the messages are mutually different (clash with one another)" • *tonikaku hanashiau koto* "at any rate the (important) thing is to talk to each other" • *sono hanashiau ba, sore jitai ga media na no da kara* "since the forum for talking together, that in itself is the media" • *kōshite* "in this way" • *Chūgoku jinmin no hitori-hitori ga tsukutta (tsukuru) media o* "the media created by Chinese citizens one by one" • *watashi ga tatte (tatsu) wa naranai to omou* "I think I must not sever" • *hatsugen de are (aru)* "whether it be a public statement" • *taido-kettei de are* "whether it be a determination of stance" • *kōdō de are* "whether it be action" • *tomokaku nani ka hannō o shinakereba* "if one doesn't at any rate show some sort of response" • *soko de media o tojiru koto ni natte shimau* "it will end in the media being closed down then and there" • *watashi mo anata mo*

❖ *tojiyō to suru mono*: ~*yō/ō to suru* = try to ~ . ❖ *koto datta no da*: for *koto*, see *Ten'anmon no koto* above; *no da* here indicates an unequivocal statement: cf. *kore wa tadashii* ("this is correct/right") and *kore wa tadashii no da*, where the latter is much more forceful. ❖ *tagai ni koto-narō to*: ~*yō/ō to* = even if ~ (= *kotonatte ite mo*). ❖ *hanashiau ba*: *ba* is used in an abstract sense here; it is roughly equivalent to *hanashiau koto* or *hanashiau chansu* (chance). ❖ *hatsugen de are*: noun + *de are* ~ noun + *de are* = whether it be ~ or ~ . ❖ *soko de*: here indicates a point in time rather than place. ❖ *hannō shitsuzukeru beki da*: verb + *beki da* = one ought to ~ .

"Both you and I" • *moshi media o tachikiritaku nakattara* "if we don't want to sever the media connections (lit., 'cut off the media')" • *ano Ten'anmon kara hasshin sareta nani ka ni hannō shitsuzukeru beki da* "we must continue responding to whatever is sent to us from Tiananmen Square" • *moshi sakoku ni iradatte (iradatsu) iru nara* "if we are fed up (lit., 'irritated') with isolationism" • *media o tsunagiawasete sekai o kaihō subeki na no da* "we should link up the media and make the world a more open place (lit., 'liberate the world')"

だ。

とてもダラダラした文章になってしまった。何回書き直してもうまく行かない。たぶん、結論めいたことを無意識に避けているのだと思う。ひたすら書き続けていないと、メディアが閉じてしまうような気がするのである。だから、ここで突然終わりたい。ここから先に書かれることは、私に連結したあなたにおまかせする。

以下余白。

• *totemo daradara shita bunshō ni natte shimatta* "this has become a very rambling piece" • *nankai kakinaoshite (kakinaosu) mo umaku ikanai* "no matter how many times I've rewritten it, it hasn't gone well" • *tabun ketsuron-meita (-meku) koto o mu-ishiki ni sakete (sakeru) iru no da to omou* "I think I may be unconsciously avoiding anything smacking of a conclusion (lit., 'anything conclusion-like; resembling a conclusion')" • *hitasura kakitsuzukete inai to* "if I don't continue writing steadfastly" • *media ga tojite shimau yō na ki ga suru no de aru* "I have the feeling that the media will be closed down" • *da kara* "that's why" • *koko de totsuzen owaritai* "here I would like to end abruptly" • *koko kara saki ni kakareru koto wa* "what is to be written from this point forward" • *watashi ni renketsu shita anata ni omakase suru* "I will leave up to you who are connected to me" • *ika yohaku* "the end (lit., 'the rest is blank')"

✤ *kaihō subeki na no da*: *subeki* derives from *suru* + *beki*; for *no da*, see *koto datta no da* above. ✤ *ketsuron-meita koto*: ~-*meku* can be added to nouns for the meaning "have the air of," "be like ~ "; -*meku* can also be used to soften an otherwise pompous-sounding expression: e.g., *tetsugaku-meita koto o itte shimatte sumimasen* ("Excuse me for sounding off like a philosopher"). ✤ *omakase suru*: the pattern *"o* + stem + *suru"* is polite (humble); *makaseru* means to entrust a duty or decision to another person. ✤ *ika yohaku*: lit., "below blank," one way of indicating the end of a written manuscript; *yohaku* = blank(s), space, margin.

Yoshimoto Banana

Yoshimoto Banana was born in 1964 in Tokyo, the daughter of the well-known poet and literary critic Yoshimoto Takaaki. A graduate of Nihon University, she became a publishing phenomenon with her first book in 1988 *Kitchen* (also available in English translation). Her straightforward tales of loneliness and coming of age, widely viewed as influenced by *manga* and film, have struck a chord with younger women readers in particular. All of her works have risen to best-seller status. Two have been made into movies—*Kitchen* and *Tsugumi*—and another, *NP*, has recently been published in English.

Yoshimoto's essay here on moments of happiness, originally published in a literary magazine, is written in a somewhat elliptical and allusive style. The note at the end discussing her motives in writing it was added by Yoshimoto on the occasion of its publication in a collection of her essays.

First published in *Bungakkai*. Copyright 1988 by Yoshimoto Banana. The essay also appears in the author's book *Painatsu purin*. Reprinted by permission of Kadokawa Shoten and the author.

幸福の瞬間

吉本ばなな

幸福とかそういうものは、本当に卵のようなものだと思う。大切だからといってきつくつかむと割れてしまうし、そっと扱いすぎても気がはってかえって負担になる。だから、古今東西何万人もの人々が語るように、いちばんよいのは、パック入り卵を自転車のかごに入れてがたがたゆらしながら無造作に帰路を急ぐおばさんのように、幸福と接することに決まっている。家に帰って、2、3個割れていても「あら、われてるわ、ま、いっか。また買えば。」と気軽に受けとめて、残りの卵を使っていればいいわけで、こういう対し方がいちばん大切である。不幸、

- *kōfuku no shunkan* "moments of happiness" • *kōfuku to ka sō iu mono wa* "such things as happiness (lit., 'happiness and the like, such things as that')" • *hontō ni* "in truth; really" • *tamago no yō na mono da to omou* "I think are something like an egg" • *taisetsu da kara to itte* "just because it is precious (i.e., valuable and easily broken)" • *kitsuku tsukamu to warete (wareru) shimau shi* "if you holds it tightly it breaks, and" • *sotto atsukaisugite (atsukau + sugiru) mo* "if you handle it too gently (i.e., with kid gloves)" • *ki ga hatte [haru]* "it's a strain (lit., 'the spirit becomes taunt')" • *kaette futan ni naru* "it becomes a burden instead"• *da kara* "that's why" • *kokon-tōzai nanman-nin mo no hitobito ga kataru yō ni* "as thousands of people have related in all ages and countries" • *ichiban yoi no wa ~ kōfuku to sessuru koto ni kimatte (kimaru) iru* "it is obvious that the best (way) of all is to associate (lit., 'come into contact') with happiness." • *pakku-iri tamago o jiten-sha no kago ni irete (ireru)* "to put a (plastic) pack of eggs in the basket of a bicycle, and" • *gatagata yurashinagara (yurasu)* "while joggling (the eggs) with a clatter" • *muzōsa ni kiro o isogu obasan no yō ni* "like a middle-aged housewife (lit., 'aunt, middle-aged woman') hurrying heedlessly home" • *ie ni kaette (kaeru)* "when reaching home" • *ni, san-ko warete (wareru) ite mo* "even if two or three are broken" • *"ara, warete 'ru (warete iru) wa, ma*

❖ *kōfuku to ka sō iu mono*: note that the author avoids commencing directly with the heavy topic of "happiness," but throws in *to ka* and *sō iu mono* to soften it. ❖ *sotto atsukaisugite mo*: stem + *sugiru* = ~ too much; *sotto* has the meanings of carefully and quietly, steathily, without touching (i.e., to leave someone alone). ❖ *kokon-tōzai*: a set expression; literally "in past and present in the East and the West"; note the reading of 今, usually read *kin*.❖ *kataru*: has the meanings of "talk; tell; speak of; relate" and indicates more serious subject matter or more considered opinion than the simple *iu* (say). ❖ *yurashinagara*: *yurasu* = to swing, rock, sway; here, of course, she is not intentionally joggling the eggs. ❖ *muzōsa*: = without particular care, attention, or thought. ❖ *kiro*: = the road home; *kiro o isogu* might be considered a set phrase. ❖ *obasan*: the image is of a busy, tough-minded, economically secure middle-aged housewife who is not to be trifled with. ❖ ~ *koto ni kimatte iru*: an idiomatic expression meaning "someone is sure to do something; something will happen without fail": e.g., *kare wa kuru koto ni kimatte iru* (He is sure to come); *kaigi wa itsumo-dōri hiraku koto ni kimatte iru* (The meeting will be held as usual without fail). ❖ *ara*: an exclamation of mild dismay or surprise; usually used by women. ❖ *warete' ru wa*: contracted form of *warete iru*; *wa* is a particle primarily used by women to express assertion or resolution in a softened form. ❖ *ma*: a colloquial abbreviation of *mā*; here indicating that though something is not sufficient, it is at a tolerable level: e.g., *Isu wa sankyaku shika nai kedo, mā ii deshō* (There are only three chairs, but oh well, I guess that's all right) ❖ *ikka*: colloquial abbreviation of *ii ka* in the form of a question to oneself; *ii* here means that there is no problem, that one does not mind about something. ❖ *mata kaeba*: short for *mata kaeba ii*. ❖ *fuzai*: note the author's use of so-called difficult words (mixed with more colloquial language) and variations on standard patterns to keep readers on their toes.

(mā), ikka (ii ka). Mata kaeba (kau)" "Oh, they're broken! Oh well, what's the difference. I can always buy some more." • *to kigaru ni uke-tomete (uketomeru)* "taking it lightly in that way" • *nokori no tamago o tsukatte (tsukau) ireba ii wake de (de aru)* "one can always use the remaining eggs (lit., 'if one uses the remaining eggs, it's all right')" • *kō iu taishikata ga ichiban taisetsu de aru* "this way of addressing (the matter) is most important"

というのはすべてほとんど、バランスの不在からやって来る。ここで言う不幸とは、外的なものではなく精神のそれです。だから私のように「幸福の瞬間」について考え込んでいるような脳みそは、あまり実際幸福とは言えない。ま、いっか。

幸福の瞬間、というのはちょっと違う気がする。過去のことはたいてい「あの日はいい日だった。」のてんこ盛りで、後になるほど美化されるものだが、その場で「死んでもいい。」と思うくらい強烈に幸福だった瞬間は再現できない、うすれてゆくばかりのものだ。その日の気候、精神、肉体両面のコンディション、人間関係、場所などすべてが重なって生み出される。私のように何となく不幸っぺえ体質の奴は〝つよさ〟を信仰する。それはいたしかたない

• *fukō to iu no wa subete* "all unhappiness" • *hotondo baransu no fuzai kara yatte kuru* "comes mostly from an absence of balance" • *koko de iu fukō to wa* "the unhappiness I am talking about here" • *gai-teki na mono de wa naku (nai)* "is not something external" • *seishin no sore desu* "it is that of the spirit" • *da kara* "that's why" • *watashi no yō ni* "like me" • *"kōfuku no shunkan" ni tsuite kangaekonde (kangaekomu) iru yō na nōmiso wa* "the type of mind that falls into thought over 'moments of happiness'" • *amari jissai kōfuku to wa ienai (iu)* "it is hard to actually call happy" • *ma (mā), ikka (ii ka)* "Well, that's the way it goes" • *kōfuku no shunkan, to iu no wa chotto chigau ki ga suru* "I feel that moments of happiness are a little different (from the above)" • *kako no koto wa* "as for the past" • *taitei* "generally" • *"ano hi wa ii hi datta" no tenkomori de (de aru)* "is heaping with many a 'That day was a good day'" • *ato ni naru hodo bika sareru mono da ga* "it (the past) is a thing that becomes idealized (lit., 'is beautified') the more time passes, but" • *sono ba de "shinde mo ii" to omou kurai kyōretsu ni kōfuku datta shunkan wa* "moments that were so intensely happy you thought you could even die on the spot" • *saigen dekinai* "cannot be recreated" • *usurete (usureru) yuku bakari no mono da* "they are things that merely fade away" • *sono hi no kikō* "the weather that day " • *seishin, nikutai ryōmen no kondishon*

❖ *sore desu*: the usage of *sore* here derives from Japanese translation of the English "that," as in the following: "The temperature of Tokyo is higher than that of Hokkaido" (*Tōkyō no kion wa Hokkaidō no sore yori takai desu*), where the natural Japanese translation would be *Tōkyō no kion wa Hokkaidō yori takai desu*; here the author uses this device for effect. ❖ *amari jissai kōfuku*: in this unusual juxtaposition of *amari* and *jissai* without particles, *jissai* can be thought of as *jissai ni wa*. ❖ *tenkomori*: an extra-large serving of food (synonymous with the broader *yamamori*); it is not usually used metaphorically. ❖ *ato ni naru hodo*: = *ato ni nareba naru hodo*. ❖ *to omou kurai kyōretsu*: here *kurai* (indicating an approximate extent or amount) is equivalent to *hodo*; "intense to the extent that you wouldn't so much mind dying." (see also *ni, san-nen kakatta kurai chikara no aru* below). ❖ *usurete yuku*: note the use of the helping verb *yuku (iku)* with abstract as well as physical motion. ❖ *fukōppē*: a coinage by Yoshimoto; *~ppē* can be added to certain nouns for the meaning of -ish (*inakappē* = a hick). ❖ *yatsu*: a colloquial, somewhat derogatory, third person pronoun; here the author gains objective distance by using it to refer to herself. ❖ *itashikata nai*: (= *shikata (ga) nai*) from the humble form of *suru*, *itashikata* is a somewhat formal, stiff expression, again exemplifying the author's mixture of styles for effect.

"mental and physical condition alike (lit., 'both aspects')" • *ningen kankei* "interpersonal relations" • *basho nado* "the physical location, etc." • *subete ga kasanatte (kasanaru) umidasareru (umidasu)* "they arise out of the combination of all of these (all combined give birth [to moments of happiness])" • *watashi no yō ni* "like me" • *nan to naku fukōppē-taishitsu no yatsu wa* "people vaguely unhappy by nature" • *"tsuyosa" o shinkō suru* "put their faith in (lit., 'worship') 'strength'" • *sore wa itashikata (= shikata) nai koto de (de aru)* "there is no help for that, and"

ことで、幸福よりも強烈なその瞬間にひかれる。若いうちだからかと思うので、まだあきらめていない。私はいつか知らない間に”卵持ってかえりおばさん”になっていたよ、というのが夢です。

私が見た、瞬間、をいくつか挙げる。

大学2年の頃、ものすごく好きになってしまった男の人がいた。今も好きだがあの頃の比ではない。ものすごく変な人で、しかも強烈な人だった。私はその人に会って、目からうろこがごろごろ落ちて、人生が変わった。彼の影響下から抜け出して自分を取り戻すのに、2、3年かかったくらい力のある人物で、彼も当時若くて支離滅裂(しりめつれつ)だったので、むちゃくちゃ楽しかった。その頃はいつも、夜明けまで大勢で飲んでいたので、記憶がむちゃくちゃだが、確

• *kōfuku yori mo kyōretsu na sono shunkan ni hikareru (hiku)* "rather than happiness I am drawn to just such moments of intensity" • *wakai uchi da kara ka to omou no de* "thinking that maybe it's because I'm still young" • *mada akiramete (akirameru) inai* "I haven't given up yet (i.e., on becoming happy in that sense)" • *watashi wa itsuka shiranai (shiru) aida ni* "some time, without realizing it (lit., 'while I don't know it')" • *"tamago motte kaeri obasan" ni natte ita yo* "I will have, hey, turned into 'the egg-carrying housewife'" • *to iu no ga yume desu* "that it is my dream" • *watashi ga mita (miru), shunkan, o ikutsu ka ageru* "I will give several of the moments I have experienced (lit., 'seen')" • *daigaku ni-nen no koro* "about my second year in college" • *monosugoku suki ni natte shimatta otoko no hito ga ita* "there was a boy I really got to like a lot" • *ima mo suki da ga* "I like him now, too, but" • *ano koro no hi de wa nai* "there is no comparison to that time" • *monosugoku hen na hito de (de aru)* "he was a very strange person" • shikamo "moreover" • *kyōretsu na hito datta* "he was an intense person" • *sono hito ni atte (au)* "meeting him" • *me kara uroko ga gorogoro ochite (ochiru)* "I suddenly saw the light (lit., 'the scales fell tumbling from my eyes'), and" • *jinsei ga kawatta (kawaru)* "my life changed" • *kare no eikyō-ka kara nukedashite (nukedasu)* "to escape from being under his influence" •

❖ *motte kaeri obasan*: *kaeri* (the noun form of *kaeru*) can be attached to other nouns (e.g., *kaeri-michi* "the road home"); here the author has coined the phrase *motte kaeri* and attached it to *obasan* (carrying-returning–housewife). ❖ *mita shunkan*: note the use of *miru* (to see or experience with all the senses) rather than *keiken suru* (experience), the former being more concrete and visual. ❖ *monosugoku*: primarily "terrifying, horrifying," now colloquial (especially among young people) for "tremendous; an awful lot." ❖ *otoko no hito*: this phrase (rather than simply *otoko*), as well as the following *sono hito* (rather than *kare*), indicates the respect the author feels for this person as well as the basic distance separating them. ❖ *hen na hito*: *hen* in this usage can be ambiguous, meaning downright peculiar or, on the other hand, eccentric in a positive sense. ❖ *me kara uroko ga (gorogoro) ochite*: a set phrase with the author's humorous addition of the rough-sounding *gorogoro* to freshen up the cliche. ❖ *shirimetsuretsu*: the basic meaning is "disorderly; incoherent," but here refers to someone who refuses to conform to convention in his lifestyle. ❖ *muchakucha tanoshikatta*: *muchakucha*: usually describes something that is confused or in disorder (as in the next sentence), but here adds the recently-developed meaning of blind or mad (*muchakucha suki da* "to be madly in love with").

---

jibun o torimodosu noni "in order to recover my selfhood" • *ni, san-nen kakatta* (kakaru) "it took two or three years" • *~ kurai chikara no aru jinbutsu de (de aru)* "he was a person with such power that ~" • *kare mo tōji wakakute shirimetsuretsu datta no de* "since he also was young and a little wild at the time" • *muchakucha tanoshikatta* "we had a great time" • *sono koro wa itsumo* "invariably in those days" • *yoake made ōzei de nonde (nomu) ita no de* "since a bunch of us drank together until dawn" • *kioku ga muchakucha da ga* "my memory of it is jumbled, but"

か、知り合って間がなかったような、気がする。そ の夜は、なぜか、みんなものすごく機嫌が良かった。 帰りようがない時刻になっていたが、もう、これ以 上飲んだら死ぬ！というような状態だった。彼は酔 った勢いで「よーし、家に行こう、みんな家に泊ま れ。」と言った。当時、私にとって彼は神だったの で、神の家に突然、おじゃまするなんて、ひええ、 であった。ギター小僧がRCのチャボに「おまえ 上手いな。」と言われるようなものであろう。神の 家には神の父、母、姉がいる。しかし当時、私には 恋とかよりも、彼の生活を見るだけで「こんなすご い人生もあるのね。」的な感動をするくらいだった ので、嬉しかった。確か女の子は私ひとりで、酔っ ぱらっていたから「家族の人に失礼な女の子だと思

• *tashika, shiriatte (shiriau) ma ga nakatta yō na, ki ga suru* "I'm pretty sure it was soon after we met" • *sono yoru wa* "that night" • *naze ka* "for some reason or other" • *minna monosugoku kigen ga yokatta* "everyone was in a great mood" • *kaeriyō ga nai jikoku ni natte ita ga* "it had reached an hour (lit., 'time') when there was no way to get home (i. e., the trains had stopped running etc.)" • *mō, kore ijō nondara (nomu) shinu!* "we would turn toes up if we drank any more!" • *to iu yō na jōtai datta* "that's the kind of condition (we were in)" • *kare wa yotta (you) ikioi de ~ to itta (iu)* "on a drunken impulse he said ~ " • *"Yōshi (yoshi), ie ni ikō (iku), minna ie ni tomare (tomaru)"* "'All right, let's go to my place, you can all stay the night at my place'" • *tōji* "at that time" • *watashi ni totte kare wa kami datta no de* "since he was a god to me" • *kami no ie ni totsuzen, ojama suru nante* "(it was) like suddenly going to visit a god's home" • *hiee, de atta* "it was Wow!" • *gitā kozō ga Āru-shī no Chabo ni ~ to iwareru (iu) yō na mono de arō* "it was like a novice guitarist being told by Chabo of RC that ~" • *"Omae umai na"* "'You are really good'"• *kami no ie ni wa kami no chichi, haha, ane ga iru* "in the god's house were also the god's father, mother, and (elder) sister" • *shikashi* "however" • *tōji* "at that time" • *watakushi ni wa* "for me" • *koi to ka yori mo* "rather than love or the like" • *kare no seikatsu o miru dake*

❖ *tashika*: means "certainly," but contains a sense of trying to recall what actually happened in the past. ❖ *kaeriyō ga nai*: = -*ō/-yō ga nai* = no way to ~ . ❖ *jikoku*: in Tokyo the buses stop running by 11:00 P.M. and the trains and subways by 12:30–1:00 A.M. ❖ *yooshi*: a lengthened version of *yoshi*; an exclamation indicating one has reached a decision, made a judgment, or arrived at an agreement. ❖ *ojama suru*: to visit (lit., "to disturb"); the set phrase *ojama shimasu* is used when one entering another person's home and *ojama shimashita* when leaving; this polite formula matches the idea of visiting the home of a god. ❖ *nante*: *nante* connects two parts of speech of equal standing, modifying what follows; equivalent to *nado to iu* and containing a sense of amazement (at the unexpectedness of it all): e.g., *Konna hoteru ni tomareru nante shiawase desu* (I'm so happy, being able to stay in a hotel like this). Here the author plays on this technique by connecting *ojama suru* with *hiee*. ❖ *hiee*: a variation of the standard *hee*, a word expressing surprise or amazement. ❖ *gitā kozō*: a *kozō* is originally a young priest or student priest and now an apprentice, an aspiring ~ , or young boy in general; usually with derogatory connotations. ❖ *RC no Chabo*: Chabo is the name of a guitarist in the rock band RC Succession. ❖ *omae*: an informal form of "you" used most often by men to other men equal or lower in status, age, etc.; can be insulting depending on the context. ❖ *umai*: the *kanji* are usually read *jōzu*; means (aside from "good-tasting") to be good at some skill or technique. ❖ *~ teki*: its function is to transform nouns into adjectives (*kōka* (effect) + *teki* = *kōka-teki* (effective); here the author has done the unusual by attaching *teki* to a whole clause; *teki na* could be replaced by *to iu fū na* with the same meaning.

---

de "just seeing how he lived" • *"konna sugoi jinsei mo aru no ne" teki na kandō o suru kurai datta no de* "I was so moved that it was like, 'Some people lead terrific lives, don't they,' and so" • *ureshikatta* "I felt happy" • *tashika onna no ko wa watashi hitori de (de aru)* "as I remember, I was the only girl, but" • *yopparatte (yopparau) ita kara "kazoku no hito ni shitsurei na onna no ko da to omowarenai (omou) ka shira" to mo omowanakatta (omou)* "since I was drunk I didn't even worry (lit., 'think') that someone in the family might think me an ill-mannered young woman"

われないかしら。」とも思わなかった。　初めて外国
へ行った日本人のようなわくわく度であった。　春で、
天気が良く、みんな夜道を大笑いして歩いて彼の家
へ向かった。　途中のコンビニエンスストアでおにぎ
りとか、おいなりさんを食べながら、とにかく楽し
いことを話して。　その時、彼が笑顔で、

「吉本、これもういっこ食べな。」

と言っておいなりさんをくれたと記憶している。
なぜこんなくだらないことをおぼえているかと言う
と、私はその時突然、深夜の住宅街で「私は今！幸
せだ。」と思ってしまったからだ。そして、その時
はっきりと、今現在幸せでしょうがないと実感した
のは、はじめてかもしれないなあ、と思ったからだ。
それ以来、実感についてよく考えるようになった

• *hajimete gaikoku e itta (iku) Nihon-jin* "a Japanese going abroad for the
first time" • *~ no yō na wakuwaku-do de atta* "I felt the same degree of
excitement as ~ " • *haru de* "it was spring" • *tenki ga yoku (yoi)* "the
weather was good" • *minna yomichi o ōwarai shite aruite (aruku)* "all of
us walked along the night streets laughing in loud voices, and" • *kare no
ie e mukatta* "we headed for his house" • *tochū no konbiniensu sutoa de*
"at a convenience store on the way" • *onigiri to ka, oinarisan o tabe-
nagara* "while eating *oinarisan* or *onigiri* or the like" • *tonikaku tanoshii
koto o hanashite (hanasu)* "anyway we talked about interesting (lit.,
'fun') things" • *sono toki* "at that time; it was then" • *kare ga egao de ~
to itte (iu)* "with a smile on his face, he said" • *"Yoshimoto, kore mō ikko
tabe [taberu] na"* "'Yoshimoto, have another one'" • *oinarisan o kureta*
"he gave me an *oinarisan*" • *to kioku shite iru* "I remember that ~" • *naze
konna kudaranai koto o oboete iru ka to iu to* "if I were to say why I
remember such a trifling thing" • *watashi wa sono toki totsuzen ~ to
omotte (omou) shimatta (shimau) kara da* "it is because suddenly at that
moment I thought ~ " • *shin'ya no jūtaku-gai de* "in a residential neigh-
borhood in the middle of the night" • *"Watashi wa ima! Shiawase da"*
"'I am happy—now!'" • *soshite ~ to omotta (omou) kara da* "and it was
also because I thought ~" • *sono toki hakkiri to* "clearly at that time" •

❖ *wakuwaku-do*: as a suffix, *do* is usually attached to nouns in the form of *kanji* compounds to show degree; here the author has not only attached it humorously to an adverb but to onomatopoeia; *wakuwaku-do* might be replaced by the much less interesting *kōfun-do* (excitement). ❖ *onigiri*: a form of rice ball enclosed in *nori*. ❖ *oinarisan*: a form of rice ball enclosed in a kind of fried tōfu. ❖ *Yoshimoto*: among friends ~*san* or ~*kun* is sometimes omitted (this is called *yobisute*); this can be an insult according to the circumstances. ❖ *naze ka to iu to ~ kara da*: a set pattern; "the reason why is ~ ." ❖ *shiawase de shō ga nai*: an idiomatic usage (~ -*te/de shō ga nai*) in which *shō (shikata) ga nai* adds the sense of "unbearably so."

---

ima genzai shiawase de (de aru) shō ga nai to jikkan shita no wa, hajimete ka mo shirenai nā "This may be the first time I've fully realized that now, this very moment, I am overwhelmingly happy" • *sore irai* "since then" • *jikkan ni tsuite yoku kangaeru yō ni natta no ka mo shirenai* "perhaps I've come to reflect a lot on (such moments of) realization"

のかもしれない。
人ごとでも、それはよいものだ。
　去年のクリスマスに、浅草で催されたコンサート
に行った帰り、バイト先にちょっと寄った。コンサ
ートにいっしょに行ったのは、バイト先の女の子達
とで、彼女達が言うには「今日、ボーナスが出た。」
だった。ウエイトレスの早番に入っていた子が、そ
の、ボーナスの入っているという、封がしてある
「茶封筒」を持っていた。開けちゃえ、と言って開
けたら1万円入っていて、びっくりした。せいぜい
2000円だろう、というおおかたの予想を裏切っ
た金額なので、喜びいさんでバイト先に私も取りに
行ってみたのだ。
　遅番に入っていたのは、某由美ちゃんだった。彼

• *hitogoto de mo* "even in regard to other people" • *sore wa yoi mono da* "that is a good thing" • *kyonen no kurisumasu ni* "at Christmas last year" • *Asakusa de moyoosareta (moyoosu) konsāto ni itta (iku) kaeri* "on my way back from a concert held in Asakusa" • *baito-saki ni chotto yotta (yoru)* "I stopped in at the place where I worked part-time" • *konsāto ni issho ni itta (iku) no wa* "(the people) I went to the concert with" • *baito-saki no onna no ko-tachi to de (de aru)* "were the girls I worked with there" • *kanojo-tachi ga iu ni wa* "what they said (lit., 'according to what they said')" • *"Kyō, bōnasu ga deta" datta* "was 'The bonus came out today'" • *ueitoresu no hayaban ni haitte (hairu) ita ko ga* "the girl who had been on the early waitress shift" • *sono ~ fū ga shite aru "cha-būtō" o motte (motsu) ita* "she had one of those ~ sealed 'brown envelopes'" • *bōnasu no haitte (hairu) iru to iu* "presumably containing (lit., 'which was said to contain') our bonuses'" • *akechae (akete [akeru] shimau)* "'Open it!'" • *to itte (iu)* "(we) told her" • *aketara ichiman-en haitte (hairu) ite* "when she opened it there was ¥10,000 inside" • *bikkuri shita* "we were surprised" • *seizei nisen-en darō* "being at most ¥2000" • *to iu ōkata no yosō o uragitta (uragiru) kingaku na no de* "since it was an amount that went against the general estimate of ~" • *yorokobiisande (yorokobi-isamu) baito-saki ni watashi mo tori ni itte (iku) mita no da* "overjoyed, I

❖ *Asakusa*: a section of Tokyo. ❖ *baito-saki*: the place where one works part-time; *baito* is from *arubaito* (part-time work, from the German "Arubeit") and *-saki* means "place" (*tsutome-saki, gaishutsu-saki,* etc.) ❖ *kanojo-tachi ga iu ni wa*: ordinarily, ~ *iu ni wa* (according to so-and-so) would be followed by *to iu koto datta* (such was the case); here the author has done without *to iu koto* for a punchier ending. ❖ *bonus*: many workers in Japan receive a base salary plus a summer and a year-end bonus whose amounts are partly based on how well the company did that year. ❖ *cha-būtō*: the cheapest type of envelope, indicating there may not be much inside. ❖ *akechae*: *-chae* = *-te shimae.* ❖ *ōkata no yosō*: a set phrase often seen in newspapers etc., providing yet another example of the author's mixing of different styles. ❖ *yosō o uragitta*: a set phrase; *uragiru* = to betray. ❖ *bō-Yumi-chan*: the use here of the rather official-sounding *bō* (a certain) and the intimate *-chan* creates an amusing contrast.

---

also went there to pick up mine" • *osoban ni haitte (hairu) ita no wa* "the person on the late shift" • *bō-Yumi-chan datta* "was a certain Yumi"

女は、すごい美人で、ものすごく気さくな、変な人である。私は店長から封筒をもらって、

「由美ちゃん、もうボーナスもらった?」

と言った。

「はい、もらいましたけど、まだ、中見てないんですよ。いくらくらいでしょうね。」

「それが、い、1万円なんだよ。これ。」

私は言った。店に客はゼロだったが、由美ちゃんはその大きな瞳(ひとみ)を見開いて、

「え——っ!」

と叫んだ。すごい、すごーい、を連発しながら、みるみるうちに顔が真赤になっていった。

「ちょうどお金がなくて困ってたんですよ〜、嬉(うれ)しい、まさかそんなにあるなんて、うわあ、オーナ

• *kanojo wa, sugoi bijin de (de aru)* "she was awfully beautiful" • *mono-sugoku kisakuna, hen na hito de aru* "she was a very open-hearted, un-usual person" • *watashi wa tenchō kara fūtō o moratte (morau)* "I received my envelope from the manager" • *"Yumi-chan, mō bōnasu moratta?" to itta (iu)* "I asked her, 'Yumi, have you gotten your bonus yet?'" • *Hai, moraimashita kedo* "Yes, I got it, but" • *mada naka mite 'nai (mite inai) n' desu yo* "I haven't looked inside yet" • *Ikura kurai deshō ne* "How much is it?" • *Sore ga, i-ichiman-en nan da yo* "It's te-ten thousand yen!" • *kore* "that's what it is" • *watashi wa itta (iu)* "I told her" • *mise ni kyaku wa zero datta ga* "there were no customers in the restaurant, and" • *Yumi-chan wa sono ōkina hitomi o mihiraite (mi-hiraku)* "Yumi opened her big eyes wide" • *"Eeeeh!" to sakenda (sake-bu)* "'What!' she cried out" • *sugoi, sugōi, o renpatsu shinagara* "while repeating 'That's great, that's great'" • *mirumiru uchi ni kao ga makka ni natte itta (iku)* "her face got redder and redder by the minute (lit., 'as we watched')" • *chōdo okane ga nakute komatte 'ta (komatte ita) n' desu yō (yo)* "it's exactly when I am broke (lit., 'troubled by not having any money')" • *ureshii* "I'm so happy" • *masaka sonna ni aru nante* "who

❖ *hen na hito*: the reason she is "strange" or "unusual" might be that she combines beauty with openheartedness. ❖ *bōnasu moratta?*: ~ *o*, indicating the direct object, is often omitted in conversation as is *ka*, indicating a question; a rising intonation makes up the difference. ❖ *kore*: usually followed by *ga*, refers back to the amount for rhetorical emphasis. ❖ *eee*: from the standard *ee*, which can express happiness, anger, suspicion, or surprise, according to context. ❖ *mirumiru uchi ni*: *mirumiru* means "before one's very eyes; suddenly"; ~ *uchi ni* = while ~ . ❖ *desu yo* ~: the squiggly line (i.e., "~") is the author's attempt to represent the intonation of *yo*, which she sees as fading and wavering. Other possibilities would be a simple よ, short and sharp, or よー, long and steady.

would have thought it was that much!" • *uwā* "Oh my!"

ーはすばらしい太っ腹だ、ああ、あんまり嬉しくて真赤になっちゃいました。」

と由美ちゃんはほっぺたを押さえて言った。私は、何か、ものすごくいいことをしたような、気がした。

別に一文も出していないのに、クリスマスだなあ、と思った。あの時、お店の中全体が、由美ちゃんの喜びでいっぱいになった瞬間を見てしまったのだ。

もうひとつ、私の家では猫を飼っている。

猫はたくさんいるのだが、なかでも特別、エビの好きな三ちゃんという奴がいて、三ちゃんにエビを見せると、明らかに他のどの時も出さない「う・わあー!」という鳴き声をする。見せた瞬間のことだ。

そして、ほら、と目の前に置いてやると必ず、いちどこちらを振りあおいで「食べてもいいの?」とい

• ōnā wa subarashī futoppara da "the owner is wonderfully big-hearted (lit., 'fat-bellied')" • ā, anmari (amari) ureshikute makka ni natchaimashita (natte shimaimashita) "Oh, I'm so happy I've turned bright red!" • to Yumi-chan wa hoppeta (= hō) o osaete (osaeru) itta (iu) "so said Yumi while pressing her cheeks" • watashi wa ~ ki ga shita "I felt as if ~" • nani ka, monosugoku ii koto o shita yō na "as if I had done something really nice" • betsu ni ichimon mo dashite (dasu) inai no ni "although I hadn't paid even a penny" • Kurisumasu da nā, to omotta "it was (like) Christmas, I thought" •あの時 ano toki "at that time" • omise no naka zentai ga "the whole restaurant" • Yumi-chan no yorokobi de ippai ni natta shunkan o mite shimatta no da "I glimpsed the moment when (the restaurant) was filled with Yumi's happiness" • mō hitotsu "one more (example)" • watashi no ie de wa neko o katte (kau) iru "we keep cats at my house" • neko wa takusan iru no da ga "there are a lot of cats, and" • naka de mo tokubetsu, ebi no suki na San-chan to iu yatsu ga ite (iru) "one of them is San-chan, who is especially fond of shrimp" • San-chan ni ebi o miseru to "when you show San-chan some shrimp" • akiraka ni hoka no dono toki mo dasanai (dasu) "U-wā!" to iu nakigoe o suru "she gives a cry, "Yeow!" which she clearly (i.e., definitely) never makes at any other time" • miseta shunkan no koto da "(it) happens the

❖ *betsu ni*: *betsu ni* + negative = nothing in particular. ❖ *ichimon*: a *mon* is an older unit of money no longer in use but still appearing in certain expressions (like "farthing" in English). ❖ *tokubetsu*: here modifies *suki*. ❖ *miseta shunkan*: i.e., "when one shows it to her"; note that the ~ta form is not always equivalent to past action; here the action is repetitive, happening every time the cat is shown the shrimp. ❖ *hora*: used to get someone's attention.

moment I show it" • *soshite* "and" • *hora, to me no mae ni oite (oku) yaru to kanarazu* "and when I set it down in front of her with a 'Here you go,' without fail" • *ichido kochira o furiaoide (furu + aogu)* "she turns and looks up and" • *"Tabete mo ii no?"* "'May I eat it?'"

う仕草（しぐさ）と表情をする。あんまり面白（おもしろ）くて、じらしたりもするが、いいよ、と言うと、すぐがつがつ食べる。何のためらいもない。幸福なお方だ。私もそんなふうにぜいたくに生きたい。

幸福の瞬間　について
いかほどに不幸な気分の人でも、ある程度は年齢が解決してくれるように思う。それはきっと、良くも悪くも自分というものの生き方のくせがわかってくるからかなあ。私自身は、17〜18の頃よりもずっと楽になった。人生は長いけれど、17くらいの頃って「今日がすべて」みたいな感じがあるから、うちに来る女子高生の手紙は、たいていつらそうなの

• to iu shigusa to hyōjō o suru "seeming to say, through her actions and expression" • anmari omoshirokute, jirashitari (jirasu) mo suru ga "it's so amusing that sometimes we tease her, but" • ii yo, to iu to "when we say, 'It's all right'" • sugu gatsugatsu taberu "she soon wolfs it down" • nan no tamerai mo nai "she doesn't hesitate at all" • kōfuku na okata da "she's a happy creature" • watashi mo sonna fū ni zeitaku ni ikitai (ikiru) "I'd like to live in luxury like that, too" • kōfuku no shunkan ni tsuite "about (the essay) "Moments of Happiness"" • ika hodo ni fukō na kibun no hito de mo "even a person of no matter how unhappy a temperament" • aru teido wa "to a certain degree" • nenrei ga kaiketsu shite kureru yō ni omou "I think that age will solve that (problem)" • sore wa kitto ~ kara ka nā "that could be because ~" • yoku mo waruku mo jibun to iu mono no ikikata no kuse ga wakatte (wakaru) kuru "for better or worse, one comes to understand the idiosyncrasies of one's own way of living" • watashi jishin wa "in my case" • jūshichi-hachi no koro yori mo zutto raku ni natta "it's much easier now than when I was seventeen or eighteen years old" • jinsei wa nagai keredo "although life is long" • jūshichi kurai no koro tte "kyō ga subete" mitai na kanji ga aru kara "since at seventeen or so one feels that 'Today is everything (i.e., everything is felt to be of earthshaking importance)'" • uchi ni kuru joshi-kōsei no

❖ *gatsugatsu*: used for eating something hungrily or greedily. ❖ *okata*: originally a very polite form for *hito;* here used humorously. ❖ *zeitaku ni ikitai*: *zeitaku* can be used for a psychological or emotional luxury which is the opposite of small-mindedness or emotional stinginess; here the author, who tends to analyze moments of happiness, is envying the cat's unthinking and unhesitating joy over the shrimp. ❖ *ika hodo ni*: = *donna ni*, but more literary. ❖ *yoku mo waruku mo*: a set phrase. ❖ *kuse*: idiosyncrasies, habits; often has a slightly negative nuance (fault, vice.) ❖ *no koro tte*: = *no koro to iu to*. ❖ *uchi ni*: one's own home and by extension oneself; in the same way *otaku* is used to refer to the home of the person being addressed and also as "you."

---

tegami wa taitei tsurasō na no de "since the letters coming to me from high school girls seem to be mostly (to be full of) suffering"

で、そういう感じを思い出すことができる。みんな、幸福でないといけない、幸福という形を追い求めることは義務である、と思っているように見える。そういう子達にこそ一瞬でも多く強烈な幸福の瞬間を知ってほしい。

• *sō iu kanji o omoidasu koto ga dekiru* "I can well remember feeling that way" • *minna ~ to omotte (omou) iru yō ni mieru* "all of them seem to think ~" • *kōfuku de nai to ikenai* "it's wrong not to be happy" • *kōfuku to iu katachi o oimotomeru (ou + motomeru) koto wa gimu de aru* "it is a duty to go after the image (lit., 'form, shape') of happiness" • *sō iu kotachi ni koso isshun de mo ōku kyōretsu na kōfuku no shunkan o shitte (shiru) hoshii* "it is just such young people that I would like to have experience (lit., 'know') many moments of intense happiness, even if (each lasts) only for an instant"

Murakami Haruki

Born in Kyoto in 1949, Murakami Haruki is a graduate of Waseda University. From 1974 to 1981 he operated a jazz coffee shop, making his literary debut in 1979 with "Hear the Wind Blow" (*Kaze no uta o kike*). He won huge popularity among younger Japanese readers with his mordant world view and wit in such novels as *Norwegian Wood* (*Noruuē no mori*), and *Dance, Dance, Dance*. Also the translator of such contemporary authors as John Irving, Raymond Carver, and Paul Theroux, Murakami has spent long periods living abroad in recent years. Several of his novels and short stories have been published in the United States, and others are available in Japan in the Kodansha English Library.

In this essay Murakami adopts a rhetorical style somewhat more difficult than his fiction (the second and third paragraphs are particularly abstract and hard to follow), but such long, embedded sentences are typical of much Japanese writing.

「狭い日本・明るい家庭」

村上春樹

このあいだ町を散歩していたら、道端に「親と子が何でも話せる楽しい家庭」という標語を書いた看板が立っていた。そーか、親と子が何でも話せると明るい家庭か、と思って何気なく通り過ぎたのだけれど、あとでなんだかその文句が妙に気になってきて（わりに細かい事が気になるたちなのだ）、翌日もう一度その看板の前を歩いて通ってみた。地元の小学生の標語コンクール入選作とある。しかしけちをつけるわけではないけれど小学生が作るにしてはどうも面白みのない標語である。月並みで、平板で、子供らしさというものがまったく感じられない。頭

• *semai Nihon* "narrow Japan (i.e., small and crowded)" • *akarui katei* "bright and cheerful homes" • *kono aida machi o sanpo shite itara* "as I was taking a walk through town the other day" • *michibata ni* "by the side of the road" • *"oya to ko ga nan de mo hanaseru tanoshii katei"* "Happy homes where parents and children can talk about anything" • *to iu hyōgo o kaita [kaku] kanban ga tatte [tatsu] ita* "there was a signboard standing (there) with that slogan written on it" • *sō ka* "is that right?" • *oya to ko ga nan de mo hanaseru to akarui katei ka to omotte [omou]* "thinking, when parents and children can talk about anything, it's a happy home, is it? • *nanige naku tōrisugita [tōrisugiru] no da* "I went on by without thinking any more about it" • *keredo, ato de nan da ka sono monku ga myō ni ki ni natte [naru] kite [kuru]* "but later on, somehow or other that phrase got strangely under my skin" • *(wari ni komakai koto ga ki ni naru tachi na no da)* "(it's in my nature to get sort of concerned about small things)" • *yokujitsu mō ichido sono kanban no mae o aruite [aruku] tōtte mita* "the next day I walked by that signboard again to check it out" • *jimoto no shōgaku-sei no hyōgo-konkūru nyūsen-saku to aru* "it turned out to be (it said that it was) the winner in a slogan contest for local elementary school students" • *shikashi* "however" • *kechi o tsukeru wake de wa nai keredo* "although I don't mean to find

❖ *semai Nihon*: the title is a play on the well-known slogan that appears later, *Semai Nihon, sonna ni isoide doko ni iku.* ❖ *kono aida*: in speech, generally pronounced *konaida*. ❖ *sō ka*: a comment to himself equivalent to *naruhodo*; the dash is to emphasize the fact that it is spoken or thought rather than "written." ❖ *nanige naku*: = *nanige nai* (lit., 'there is no spirit whatever'), meaning without thought, particular intention, or special attention. ❖ *nan da ka.* = for some unclear reason; roughly equivalent to *nan to naku.* ❖ *monku*: can also mean "complaint; gripe." ❖ *ki ni natte kita*: *ki ni naru* = can't keep off one's mind, be bothered by, get on one's nerves; *kita*, from *kuru*, indicates that a condition has reached a certain stage: e.g., *nemuku natte kita* might be translated as "I've gotten sleepy; I've started to feel sleepy." ❖ *wari ni*: with the primary meaning of "relatively," modifies the following *ki ni naru.* ❖ *tachi*: colloquial for nature, disposition, temperament (or quality when referring to objects). ❖ *tōtte mita*: *-te miru* is usually translated "to try -ing," but here the meaning is closer to "to do and see what would happen.". ❖ *nyūsen-saku to aru*: in this case *to aru* = *to kaite aru* or, less explicitly, that it was somehow otherwise indicated. ❖ *kechi o tsukeru*: a set expression; *kechi* originally meant bad luck or an ill omen and retains vestiges of that meaning in some usages. ❖ *ni shite wa*: "considering the fact that"; note that in this phrase *ni* can follow a verb. ❖ *dōmo*: followed by a negative, means that no matter how one's tries, thinks, or looks at something, the negative conclusion is inevitable; here roughly equivalent to *dō mite mo* or *dō kangaete mo.*

---

fault" • *shōgaku-sei ga tsukuru ni shite wa dōmo omoshiromi no nai hyōgo de aru* "for something written by an elementary school student, the slogan was somehow without much interest" • *tsukinami de [de aru]* "it was trite" • *heiban de [de aru]* "it was flat (dull)" • *kodomo-rashisa to iu mono ga mattaku kanjirarenai [kanjiru]* "one could not feel anything childlike (in it) at all"

の中でこねて、ただ単語をならべて作っただけの空しい文章である。もちろん作る子供よりは、こういうものを選ぶ教師のほうに問題があることは言うまでもない。こういうものを選ぶ教師の価値観に子供が迎合しちゃうのである。情けないことに。

それはともかく、親と子が何でも話せる家庭というのは本当に楽しい家庭なんだろうか？ と僕はその標語の前に立って、根本的に考えこんでしまう。

こういう標語は時として根本的な思考の確認を迫ることがある。僕は思うのだけれど、家庭というのはこれはあくまで暫定的な制度である。それは絶対的なものでもないし、確定的なものでもない。はっきり言えば、それは通りすぎていくものである。不断に変化し移りゆくものである。そしてその暫定性の

• *atama no naka de konete [koneru]* "it was shaped (lit., 'kneaded') inside the head" • *tada tango o narabete [naraberu] tsukutta [tsukuru] dake no munashii bunshō de aru* "it was nothing more than an empty phrase made by stringing words together" • *mochiron* "of course" • *tsukuru kodomo yori wa* "more than the child who made it" • *kō iu mono o erabu kyōshi no hō ni mondai ga aru* "the problem is rather with the educators who choose this kind of thing" • *koto wa iu made mo nai* "it goes without saying that ~ " • *kō iu mono o erabu kyōshi no kachi-kan ni kodomo ga geigō shichau [shite shimau] no de aru* "the children end up catering to the values of the educators who choose works like this" • *nasakenai koto ni* "sad as it is" • *sore wa tomokaku* "be that as it may" • *oya to ko ga nan de mo hanaseru katei to iu no wa hontō ni tanoshii katei nan darō ka?* "is a home where parents and children can talk about anything really a happy home?" • *to boku wa ~ konpon-teki ni kangaekonde [kangaekomu] shimau* "I pondered the fundamental question of whether ~" • *sono hyōgo no mae ni tatte [tatsu]* "(while) standing in front of that slogan" • *kō iu hyōgo wa* "this sort of slogan" • *toki toshite* "there are times when (i.e., depending on the situation)" • *konponteki na shikō no kakunin o semaru koto ga aru* "one is pressed to confirm one's fundamental thinking" • *boku wa omou no da keredo* "to my way of thinking"

❖ *geigō shichau*: *shichau* = *shite shimau*; *-te shimau* here indicates that an action has been brought to an end, but also that there is an element of disappointment in or disapproval of the result. ❖ *nasakenai*: originally *nasake* (pity) + *nai* (without); here meaning "regrettable"; note that the phrase is an example of inversion, modifying the preceding *geigō shichau*. ❖ *sore wa tomokaku*: a set phrase (sometimes followed by *toshite*) meaning "however that may be" (*tomokaku* = "at any rate," "anyhow," "apart from"). ❖ *katei to iu no wa*: *to iu no wa* here, and in innumerable instances below, sets off the preceding noun as a subject of general discussion, not a particular case. ❖ *boku*: "I"; male usage generally on a somewhat lower politeness level than *watashi* or *watakushi*; in this paragraph, the author repeatedly uses *boku* to emphasize that he is stating a personal opinion. ❖ *kangaekonde*: *komu* (roughly, to enter or put in), is attached to verb stems to indicate that something is done fully or thoroughly: e.g., *nomikomu* (to swallow), *omoikomu* (to be occupied by an idea), *shinjikomu* (to be a firm believer). ❖ *boku wa omou no da keredo*: a common way of broaching a subject; another possibility is *boku no kangae da wa*. ❖ *katei to iu no wa kore wa*: *kore* wa (which equals *katei to iu no wa*) is used here for stress. ❖ *hakkiri ieba*: other variations on the ~ *ieba* formula are *teinei ni ieba* (to put it politely) and *ōzappa ni ieba* (broadly speaking). ❖ *tōrisugite iku*: *sugiru* here means "go by; go past" rather than "to go to an extreme."

• *katei to iu no wa* "what we call a family" • *kore wa akumade zantei-teki na seido de aru* "this is strictly a provisional system" • *sore wa zettai-teki na mono de mo nai shi* "it is not an absolute thing, and" • *kakutei-teki na mono de mo nai* "it is not a fixed thing either" • *hakkiri ieba* "frankly speaking" • *sore wa tōrisugite [tōrisugiru] iku mono de aru* "it is something that is passed through" • *fudan ni henka shi [suru] utsuriyuku mono de aru* "it is something that is perpetually changing and shifting" • *soshite* "and"

危うさを認識することによって、家庭はその構成員のそれぞれの自我をソフトに吸収していくことができる。それがなければ、家庭というものはただの無意味な硬直した幻想でしかない。家庭というのは、いわばソフトに作られた自我のゼロサム社会なのである。僕は個人的にそう考えている。だから親と子が何でも正直に包み隠すことなく喋って、そうすることによって家庭が初めて健全になるというのは、あまりにも単純で一面的な発想だと思う。

もちろん家族全員が疑心暗鬼であったりするとそれはたしかにまずいだろうとは思うけれど、少しくらいお互いに秘密があったっていいじゃないか。口に出すべきことと、出すべきではないこととをきちんと識別する能力というのは、自我の社会化にとっ

• *sono zantei-sei no ayausa [ayaui = abunai] o ninshiki suru koto ni yotte* "by means of recognizing (lit., 'being aware of') the precariousness of that provisional nature" • *katei wa ~ o sofuto ni kyūshū shite iku koto ga dekiru* "the family can softly (flexibly) assimilate ~" • *sono kōsei-in no sorezore no jiga o* "the respective egos of the (family) members" • *sore ga nakereba* "if that were not the case" • *katei to iu mono wa* "the family" • *tada no mu-imi na kōchoku shita gensō de [de aru] shika nai* "would be nothing but a meaningless, inflexible illusion" • *katei to iu no wa* "the family" • *iwaba sofuto ni tsukurareta [tsukuru] jiga no zero-samu shakai na no de aru* "we could say (in a manner of speaking) it is a flexibly created 'zero-sum society of egos'" • *kojin-teki ni* "personally" • *sō kangaete [kangaeru] iru* "that's what I believe" • *dakara* "that's why" • *oya to ko ga nan de mo shōjiki ni tsutsumikakusu koto naku shabette [shaberu]* "parents and children talking honestly about everything without concealing anything" • *sō suru koto ni yotte* "by doing so" • *katei ga hajimete kenzen ni naru to iu no wa* "(the notion) that a home for the first time becomes healthy" • *amari ni mo tanjun de [de aru] ichimen-teki na hassō da to omou* "I think that way of thinking is just too simple-minded and one-sided" • *kazoku zen'in ga gishin-anki de attari suru to* "if all the family members are suspicious of each other or whatever" • *sore wa*

❖ *shika nai*: "is nothing but ~ ." ❖ *iwaba*: "so to speak; as it were"; a common connective. ❖ *nan de mo shōjiki ni tsutsumikakusu koto naku shabette*: *nan de mo shōjiki ni* is modifying *shabette*, as is of course *tsutsumikakusu koto naku*. ❖ *hajimete kenzen ni naru*: here *hajimete* means "finally" or "at last" after passing through a specific experience. ❖ *amari ni mo*: the set phrase *amari ni* ("too, such") plus *mo* for emphasis. ❖ *gishin-anki*: lit., "doubting-heart darkness-goblin"; from the Buddhist saying *Gishin anki o shōzu* 疑心暗鬼を生ず (Suspicion gives birth to bogies). ❖ *de attari suru*: the use of *~tari* indicates other possibilites. ❖ *mazui*: (lit., "bad tasting"), often used in this sense of *ikenai* (it won't do); the colloquial usage makes it stand out in the present context. ❖ *sukoshi kurai*: = a little, a few; here *kurai* has the rough meaning of "about; approximately," showing extent or amount. ❖ *himitsu ga atta tte*: roughly equivalent to *himitsu ga atte mo*. ❖ *dasu beki*: ~ *beki* = ought to ~ .

---

tashika ni mazui darō to wa omou keredo "I think that that certainly wouldn't do, but" • *sukoshi kurai otagai ni himitsu ga atta tte ii ja nai ka* "(I also think that) isn't it all right for them to have a few secrets from each other?" • *kuchi ni dasu beki koto to dasu beki de wa nai koto to* "things that should be put into words and things that should not be put into words" • ~ *to* ~ *to o kichinto shikibetsu suru nōryoku* "the ability to clearly distinguish ~ from ~ "

てはけっこう重要な能力であるはずだ。何でも話せるのが善という発想はいささか強引すぎると思うし、それは本来的に家庭が有しているべきソフトさを考慮に入れていない。そういう考えを抱くこと自体を僕は否定しようとは思わないが（それはもちろん個人の自由である）、標語にして押しつけるのはどうかと思う。

まあそれはともかく、しばらく外国で暮らして戻ってくると、日本というのは本当に標語が好きな国なんだなあと感心する。外国では標語というのはまず見かけない。こんなに標語が多いのは、僕が知っているかぎりでは日本くらいである。そう思って改めてまわりを見回すと、日本全国隅から隅までびっしりと標語だらけである。それもいったいこれが何

• ~ *nōryoku to iu no wa jiga no shakai-ka ni totte wa kekkō jūyō na nōryoku de aru hazu da* "the ability to ~ must be regarded as (lit., 'should be') a pretty important ability in the socialization of the ego" • *nan de mo hanaseru no ga zen to iu hassō wa* "the idea (lit., 'way of thinking') that being able to talk about anything is a virtue" • *isasaka gōin-sugiru to omou shi* "I think it is a bit forced, and" • *sore wa honrai-teki ni katei ga yūshite [yūsuru = aru] iru beki sofutosa o kōryo ni irete [ireru] inai* "that does not take into account the softness that a family should fundamentally (lit., 'originally') possess" • *sō iu kangae o idaku koto jitai o boku wa hitei shiyō to wa omowanai [omou] ga* "I have no intention of denying the right of people to think in that way, but (lit., 'I am not thinking of trying to deny the holding of such an idea in itself, but')" • (*sore wa mochiron kojin no jiyū de aru*) "(that is, of course, a matter of personal freedom)" • *hyōgo ni shite oshitsukeru no wa dō ka to omou* "I do have doubts about making it into a slogan and forcing it (on people)" • *mā sore wa tomokaku* "well, setting aside that matter" • *shibaraku gaikoku de kurashite [kurasu] modotte [modoru] kuru to* "when I come back (to Japan) after living abroad for some time" • *Nihon to iu no wa hontō ni hyōgo ga suki na kuni nan da nā to kanshin suru* "I am amazed by how very fond this country Japan is of slogans" • *gaikoku*

❖ *kekkō jūyō na*: here *kekkō* (more broadly, "good; fine" or a polite rejection in the sense of "I'm fine") here is the more colloquial "fairly; pretty much." ❖ *isasaka*: "a little; somewhat." ❖ *hitei shiyō to wa omowanai*: *~ō/~yō to omou* = intend to ~; *~ō/yō to wa omowanai* = do not intend to ~ . ❖ *dō ka to omou*: a phrase used to doubt the wisdom of something. ❖ *kanshin suru*: primarily means "to be impressed," but here, ironically, "to be astonished or astounded" at some stupidity. ❖ *mazu mikakenai*: *mazu*, with the primary meaning of "first of all," means "almost" in this usage when followed by a negative. ❖ *Nihon kurai*: *kurai*, which has the common meaning of "about" or "approximately" when referring to amounts, here is setting up a standard of comparison: e.g., *konna koto shitte iru no wa kanojo kurai darō* (she is about the only one who knows this). ❖ *sumi kara sumi made*: lit., "from corner to corner (as in a room)"; a set phrase. ❖ *hyōgo darake*: *darake* indicates that a preceding noun is full of or covered with something undesirable: e.g., *kare no kōto wa doro darake da* (his coat is covered with mud). ❖ *ittai*: (originally, "one body; one whole"), is used when questioning the validity of something said or, as here, expressing a doubt: similar to "what in the world; what on earth."

---

de wa hyōgo to iu no wa mazu mikakenai [mikakeru] "one isn't likely to come across slogans in foreign countries" • *konna ni hyōgo ga ōi no wa, ~ Nihon kurai de aru* "Japan is about the only place ~ that has so many slogans" • *boku ga shitte [shiru] iru kagiri de wa* "as far as I know" • *sō omotte [omou] aratamete mawari o mimawasu to* "when one looks around once more with this in mind" • *Nihon zenkoku sumi kara sumi made bisshiri to hyōgo darake de aru* "from end to end, the whole of Japan is positively jam-packed with slogans" • *sore mo* "and even those (i.e., the slogans)" • *ittai kore ga nan no yaku ni tatsu no darō ka* "what purpose in the world does it (lit., 'this') serve?"

の役に立つのだろうかと首をひねりたくなる不思
議・不可解なものが多い。役に立たないばかりでは
なく、その多くは非論理的であり、文章としての品
位に欠けている。たとえばこの「親と子が云々」の
標語にしたって、こんな看板を道端に立ててそれで
何か効果があると思いますか？　この看板を見た人
がそれによって善導されるような状況が生じる可能
性があると思いますか？　僕はないと思う。そりゃ
世の中にはいろんな人がいるから十万にひとつくら
いはそういうこともあるかもしれない。でもそれだ
けのためにわざわざ小学生を集めてコンクールを開
くこともないだろう。まったく無意味だと僕は思う。
丸谷才一氏がどこかで小学生に詩を書かせることの
無意味さについて書いておられたけれど、小学生に

• *to kubi o hineritaku naru fushigi-fukakai na mono ga ōi* "many of them
are so strange and incomprehensible that it makes you think (lit., 'that
you want to crane your neck [in puzzlement]')" • *yaku ni tatanai [tatsu]
bakari de wa naku* "not only do they not serve any purpose (but)" • *sono
ōku wa hironri-teki de ari [de aru]* "most of them are illogical" • *bunshō
toshite no hin'i ni kakete [kakeru] iru* "they are lacking in style (lit.,
'dignity') as writing" • *tatoeba* "for example" • *kono "oya to ko ga
unnun" no hyōgo ni shita tte* "even taking the slogan 'Parents and children etc.'" • *konna kanban o michibata ni tatete [tateru] sore de nani ka
kōka ga aru to omoimasu ka?* "do you really think putting up this kind of
signboard on the roadside is going to have any effect?" • *kono kanban o
mita hito ga* "people who have seen this sign" • *sore ni yotte* "because of
that" • *zendō sareru yō na jōkyō ga shōjiru kanō-sei ga aru to omoimasu
ka?* "do you think that there is any possibility that a situation will arise
such as to lead (people who have seen this sign) onto the right path?" •
boku wa nai to omou "I don't think so" • *sorya [sore wa]* "even so" • *yo
no naka ni wa ironna [iroiro na] hito ga iru kara* "because there are all
kinds of people in the world" • *jūman ni hitotsu kurai wa sō iu koto mo
aru ka mo shirenai* "that kind of thing might happen in something like
one out of 100,000 (cases)" • *de mo sore dake no tame ni* "but, just for

❖ *yaku ni tatanai bakari de wa naku*: ~ *bakari de wa naku* = not only is it ~ but it is ~ . ❖ *hyōgo ni shita tte*: ~ *ni suru* means roughly to pick out and decide upon something; *shita tte* is the somewhat more emphatic equivalent of *shite mo*. ❖ *to omoimasu ka*: here the author turns to address the reader directly, and continues more or less to do so until somewhere around the middle of the following paragraph. ❖ *sorya [sore wa]*: indicates that the author has had second thoughts. ❖ *wazawaza*: means to do something especially (to go out of one's way), not incidentally. ❖ *hiraku koto mo nai darō*: ~ *koto mo nai darō* = ~ing is uncalled for; isn't it better not to ~ ?; *koto* here means "need; necessity." ❖ *Maruya Saiichi*: a well-known Japanese novelist and literary critic. ❖ *kaite orareta*: *oru* is here used as the polite form of *iru*.

---

the sake of that" • *wazawaza shōgaku-sei o atsumete konkūru o hiraku koto mo nai darō* "there is no need to go to the trouble of rounding up elementary school children and holding a contest" • *mattaku mu-imi da to boku wa omou* "I think it is absolutely meaningless" • *Maruya Saiichi-shi ga doko ka de ~ kaite [kaku] orareta [oru] keredo* "Maruya Saiichi wrote somewhere that ~ , but" • *shōgaku-sei ni shi o kakaseru koto no mu-imisa ni tsuite* "about the meaninglessness of having elementary school students write poetry"

標語を作らせるというのもそれにまけず劣らず無意味ではないかと思う。

それから道を歩いていてよく見かけるあの「世界人類が平和でありますように」という標語看板、あれも僕にはよくわからないです。全然理解できない。もちろん僕だって世界人類が平和であってほしいとは思う。そういう意味では標語の趣旨そのものには異論はない。まああえて言うなら、「じゃあ何か、地球が良きゃ宇宙はどうなってもいいのか？」ということになるわけだが、これはいささかからみすぎという気がしないでもない。だからまあ趣旨には根本的に賛同する。問題はそんな看板をいちいち日本国中に立ててまわっていったいどのような具体的効果があるのか、ということである。その標語を見た

• *shōgaku-sei ni hyōgo o tsukuraseru [tsukuru] to iu no mo* "having elementary school students make slogans, also" • *sore ni makezu [makeru; makenaide] otorazu [otoru; otoranaide] mu-imi de wa nai ka to omou* "is not far behind that, I think, in meaninglessness" • *sorekara* "and (then)" • *michi o aruite [aruku] ite yoku mikakeru* "(the signboard) you often come across while walking along the street" • *ano "Sekai-jinrui ga heiwa de arimasu yō ni" to iu hyōgo kanban* "that (well-known) signboard saying, "May peace prevail on earth" (lit., 'so that the people of the world will be at peace')" • *are mo boku ni wa yoku wakaranai desu* "that doesn't make sense to me either" • *zenzen rikai dekinai* "I can't understand it at all" • *mochiron* "of course" • *boku datte* "even I (i.e., I as much as anyone else)" • *sekai-jinrui ga heiwa de atte hoshī to wa omou* "I do want all the peoples of the world to be at peace" • *sō iu imi de wa* "in that sense" • *hyōgo no shushi sono mono ni wa iron wa nai* "I have no objection as concerns the slogan's sentiment (lit., 'aim, purpose') in itself" • *mā* "well" • *aete iu nara* "if I may be so bold as to say" • *"Jā nani ka, chikyū ga yokya [yokereba] uchū wa dō natte mo ii no ka?"* "Then you mean, if the Earth is OK, it doesn't matter what happens to the universe?" • *to iu koto ni naru wake da ga* "it becomes a matter of" • *kore wa isasaka karamisugi [karamu + sugiru] to iu ki ga shinai de mo*

MURAKAMI HARUKI 144

❖ *[sore ni] makezu-otorazu*: a set phrase meaning "equally" (lit., "not being defeated by and not being inferior to ~ in ~"). ❖ *de wa nai ka to omou*: roughly, "I wonder if it is not a case of ~." *mikakeru*: the phrase ending with *mikakeru* modifies the following noun phrase concluding in *kanban*. ❖ *ano*: = "that"; the use of *ano* indicates some shared knowledge and piques the reader's interest in what is to follow; the later *are mo* also shows information held in common (*sore mo* would not be possible). ❖ *"Sekai-jinrui ga heiwa de arimasu yō ni"*: a sticker that many Japanese have put up outside their homes (in a campaign sponsored by Sasakawa Ryōichi). ❖ *aete iu nara*: *aete* means "boldly," "daringly"; it is often used rhetorically in this way (venture to ~, be so bold as to ~). ❖ *nani ka*: here used rhetorically to mean "Do you mean to say"; roughly equivalent to *sore de wa*. ❖ *to iu ki ga shinai de mo nai*: this use of a double negative to express something partially positive is quite common in Japanese.

---

nai "I can't help feeling that I may be going a little out of my way to be difficult here, but" • *dakara* "so" • *mā shushi ni wa konpon-teki ni sandō suru* "I suppose I am basically in agreement with the sentiment" • *mondai wa ~ to iu koto de aru* "the problem is ~ " • *sonna kanban o ichi-ichi Nihon kokujū ni tatete [tateru] mawatte [mawaru]* "when (they) go all around Japan putting up such signboards one by one" • *ittai dono yō na gutai-teki kōka ga aru no ka* "for God's sake, what kind of concrete effect is there?"

人々の頭に「世界人類が平和でありますように」という主張がインプットされて、それに従って人々が行動し、その結果世界に平和が訪れ、人類が幸せになるなどということが可能性としてあるだろうか？

それはないですね。断言してもいい。そんなことは絶対にありえない。何故ならこの世の中に世界人類が平和であってほしくないと望んでいる人なんてまずいないだろうし（もしいたとしてもそういう人が看板を目にして「そうだ、世界人類は平和でなくちゃいけないんだ」と悟って改心するようなことはまずあるまい）、それが頭にインプットされたからといってそれによって新たな具体的な効果が生じるなんてことはありえないからである。たとえば極端な話、ヒットラーにしたってある狭い意味においては

• *sono hyōgo o mita hitobito no atama ni* "into the heads of the people who see that slogan" • *"Sekai-jinrui ga heiwa de arimasu yō ni" to iu shuchō ga inputto sarete* "the assertion "May peace prevail on earth" is input" • *sore ni shitagatte [shitagau] hitobito ga kōdō shi [suru]* "people act in accordance with that" • *sono kekka sekai ni heiwa ga otozure [otozureru]* "as a result peace comes to (lit., 'visits') the world" • *jinrui ga shiawase ni naru nado* "humanity becomes happy etcetera" • *to iu koto ga kanō-sei toshite aru darō ka?* "is there any possibility of ~ ? (lit., 'does this type of thing exist as a possibility?')" • *sore wa nai desu ne* "no, there isn't" • *dangen shite mo ii* "I am willing to state that categorically" • *sonna koto wa zettai ni arienai [aru + eru]* "that is absolutely impossible" • *naze nara ~ kara de aru* "that is because ~" • *kono yo no naka ni* "in this world" • *sekai-jinrui ga heiwa de atte hoshiku nai to nozonde [nozomu] iru hito nante mazu inai darō shi* "there isn't likely anyone who doesn't wish for humanity to be at peace, and" • *(moshi ita to shite mo* "even if there should be" • *sō iu hito ga kanban o me ni shite* "such a person, seeing the signboard," • *"Sōda, sekai-jinrui wa heiwa de nakucha [nakute wa] ikenai n da" to satotte [satoru] kaishin suru* "[thinks; or says] 'Of course, the peoples of the world must live in peace,' realizes the errors of his ways (lit., 'is enlightened') and has a

❖ *arienai*: "cannot exist," "is impossible"; a compound of *aru + eru*. ❖ *sekai-jinrui ga heiwa de atte hoshiku nai*: *~te hoshī* = want (someone else) to ~ . ❖ *me ni shite*: *me ni suru* = to see physically, i.e., to see with one's own eyes. ❖ *aru mai*: verb + *mai* = it is doubtful that ~; when used with an intensifier as it is here (*mazu*), *mai* stresses that something won't happen. ❖ *inputto sareta kara to itte*: = *to itte* = even though ~ . ❖ *kyoku-tan na hanashi*: this set phrase could be followed by *toshite* ("as"), but it is stronger standing alone; a common rhetorical device in Japanese.

---

change of heart" • *~ yō na koto wa mazu aru mai*) "there is little likeli-hood that ~ is going to happen" • *sore ga atama ni inputto sareta kara to itte [iu]* "just because that [slogan] is input into his head" • *sore ni yotte* "because of that" • *arata na gutai-teki na kōka ga shōjiru nante koto wa arienai* "it is impossible that any new, concrete effect will be produced" • *tatoeba* "for example" • *kyokutan na hanashi* "(as) an extreme case" • *Hittorā ni shita tte* "take even Hitler" • *aru semai imi ni oite wa* "in a narrow sense"

世界人類が平和であることを望んでいた。ただ彼はゲルマン＝アーリア民族のファナティックな価値観主導のもとにそれがなされるべきだと考えていたので、当たり前のことながら戦争になってしまった。世界認識そのものが狂っていただけなのだ。

要するに僕が言いたいのは、人々に世界平和を望ませればそれで事足るというものではないということである。必要なのは共通した世界認識と、もっと具体的な細かい行動原則である。それがなければ、何も始まらない。

僕はそういうタイプの行動原則のない茫漠とした（しかしとりたてて反論のしようのない）主張を「ウルトラマン的主張」と呼んでいる。ウルトラマンならそれを目にとめて「そうだ、世界人類を平和

• *sekai-jinrui ga heiwa de aru koto o nozonde [nozomu] ita* "he hoped for the world's peoples to be at peace" • *tada ~ no de* " but since" • *kare wa* "he" • *Geruman-Āria-minzoku no fanatikku na kachikan shudō no moto ni* "under the leadership of a fanatic German=Aryan value system" • *sore ga nasareru [nasu] beki da to kangaete [kangaeru] ita* "he thought that that (i. e., world peace) should be carried out" • *atarimae no koto nagara* "as a natural course of events" • *sensō ni natte shimatta* "war broke out" • *sekai ninshiki sono mono ga kurutte [kuruu] ita dake na no da* "it was just that his perception of the world, in and of itself, was warped (lit., 'had gone awry; was crazed')" • *yōsuru ni* "in short" • *boku ga iitai [iu + tai] no wa ~ to iu koto de aru* "what I want to say is ~ " • *hitobito ni sekai heiwa o nozomasereba [nozomu]* "even if you cause people to want world peace" • *sore de kototaru to iu mono de wa nai* "that will not in itself be sufficient" • *hitsuyō na no wa ~ de aru* "what is necessary is ~" • *kyōtsū shita sekai ninshiki to* "a common (i.e., shared) world perception and" • *motto gutai-teki na komakai kōdō-gensoku* "a more concrete and elaborate code of behavior" • *sore ga nakereba* "without that" • *nani mo hajimaranai* "nothing can be achieved; the situation is hopeless (lit., 'nothing begins')" • *sō iu taipu no kōdō-gensoku no nai bōbaku to shita ~ shuchō o* "statements ~ of this type, sweeping and

❖ *toritatete*: "in particular." ❖ *shiyō no nai*: *shiyō ga nai* (*ga* here replaced by *no*) is a set phrase meaning that there is no way of doing or accomplishing something. ❖ *Ultraman*: the hero of a Japanese children's TV show launched in 1966 and a Superman-like figure working to right the world's wrongs. ❖ *heiwa ni shinakucha*: = *heiwa ni shinakute wa ikenai*.

---

without a code of behavior" • *(shikashi toritatete hanron no shiyō no nai)* "but which cannot be taken up specifically and refuted" • *"Uru-toraman-teki shuchō" to yonde [yobu] iru* "I call them "Ultraman-like statements" • *Urutoraman nara* "if it were Ultraman" • *sore o me ni tomete* "he would spot them" • *"Sō da, sekai-jinrui o heiwa ni shi-nakucha [shinakute wa]"* "That's right! One must bring peace to the peoples of the world."

にしなくちゃ」と決意を新たにするだろうが、それ以外には何の効果もないという意味である。しかしこういうタイプの標語はまあ実に多い。うんざりするほど多い。「犯罪のない明るい社会を」だとか、「目標・交通事故死ゼロ」なんて、いったい何のためにこんな看板わざわざ出しているのか僕にはもう全然見当がつかない。見ているだけで馬鹿馬鹿しくなってくる。ただ資源と人手を無駄に費やし、街を汚しているだけである。

あと多いのはお節介標語で、これも大変に見苦しい。たとえばいちばん有名な「狭い日本、そんなに急いでどこにいく」だって、これは本当によけいな御世話だと思う。だいたい日本が狭いなんて誰が決めたんだろう。そうでしょう、日本というのはそれ

• *~ to ketsui o arata ni suru darō ga* "he would probably renew his determination that ~ , but" • *sore igai ni wa nan no kōka mo nai* "there is no effect whatsoever other than that" • *~ to iu imi de aru* "that's what I mean (by calling it an Ultraman-like statement)" • *shikashi* "however" • *kō iu taipu no hyōgo wa mā jitsu ni ōi* "there are, well, really a lot of slogans of this type" • *unzari suru hodo ōi* "they are sickeningly numerous" • *"hanzai no nai akarui shakai o" da to ka* "for example '[Let's make] a bright and cheerful society without crime'" • *"Mokuhyō: kōtsū jiko-shi zero" nante* "or something like 'Objective: zero deaths in traffic accidents'" • *ittai nan no tame ni konna kanban wazawaza dashite [dasu] iru no ka* "for what earthly purpose do (they) go to all the trouble of putting out such signs?" • *boku ni wa mō zenzen kentō ga tsukanai [tsuku]* "I really can't imagine at all" • *mite [miru] iru dake de* "at just the sight of them" • *bakabakashiku natte kuru* "it gets ridiculous" • *tada ~ dake de aru* "it is nothing more than ~" • *shigen to hitode o muda ni tsuiyashi [tsuiyasu]* "it is a waste of natural resources and human effort" • *machi o yogoshite iru* "it is defiling the town" • *ato ōi no wa osekkai hyōgo de [de aru]* "also numerous are officious slogans" • *kore mo taihen ni migurushii* "these are also extremely ugly to see" • *tatoeba ~ datte* "take ~ for example" • *ichiban yūmei na* "the most famous" • *"Semai Nihon, sonna*

❖ *mā jitsu ni ōi*: *mā* is an exclamation with a colloquial feeling. ❖ *unzari [suru]*: used when one is tired of or fed up with something. ❖ *mō zenzen kentō ga tsukanai*: here, *mō* is an exclamation indicating slight disapproval or admonishment. ❖ *ato*: usually "afterward," here means "the rest." ❖ *osekkai*: refers to meddling, sticking one's nose into other people's business. ❖ *yokei na osewa da*: a set phrase indicating that it is none of your business (lit., "unwarranted care"); *ōkina osewa da* is used in the same way. ❖ *daitai*: an intensifier with such meanings as "in general," "in the first place," and "whatever; whoever."

---

ni isoide [isogu] doko ni iku ""(In) "narrow" Japan, where are you going in such a hurry?"" • *kore wa hontō ni yokei na osewa da to omou* "I really think that is just meddling in other people's business" • *daitai ~ dare ga kimeta [kimeru] n' darō* "whoever decided that ~ ?" • *Nihon ga semai nante* "as for something like Japan being narrow" • *sō deshō* "don't you agree" • *Nihon to iu no wa* "this country Japan"

はシベリアとかサハラ砂漠に比べればそれは狭いだろう。でも僕の実感からすればかなり広い国である。東京だってずいぶん広い街である。山手線の駅だってまだ下りたことのない駅がけっこうある。それをのっけから狭い日本なんて言われるとまずひっかかる。認識が一面的である。それから狭い国の国民が急いじゃいかんのかという問題もある。誰だってどこに住んでいようが、急ぐことはある。そういう時には誰がなんと言おうと道は長く、世界は広く感じられる。もちろん車が無用のスピードを出すことには僕も反対だけれど、だからといってこういう奇妙な言語感覚の看板を世間に撒きちらしていいものだろうか？　この手のお節介看板は警察関係がいちばん多いように思う。その殆どはすくいようがなく奇

• *sore wa Shiberia to ka Sahara-sabaku ni kurabereba [kuraberu]* "when it's compared to Siberia or the Sahara Desert" • *sore wa semai darō* "it *is* narrow" • *de mo* "however" • *boku no jikkan kara sureba [suru]* "from my own sense of things" • *kanari hiroi kuni de aru* "it is quite a big country" • *Tōkyō datte* "take Tokyo" • *zuibun hiroi machi de aru* "it is a very large city" • *Yamanote-sen no eki datte* "take Yamanote line stations" • *mada orita [ariru] koto no nai eki ga kekkō aru* "there are many stations I've never been to (lit., 'gotten off at')" • *sore o nokke kara* "(being told) that out of the blue" • *semai Nihon nante iwareru [iu] to* "when I hear 'Japan narrow' etc." • *mazu hikkakaru* "it sticks in my craw (lit., 'I get hung-up right there')" • *ninshiki ga ichimen-teki de aru* "that way of thinking (lit., 'perception') is one-sided" • *sore kara* "and also" • *semai kuni no kokumin ga isoija [isoide wa] ikan [ikenai] no ka* "is it wrong for the citizens of a narrow country to hurry?" • *to iu mondai mo aru* "there is also the problem of ~" • *dare datte* "anyone, no matter who" • *doko ni sunde [sumu] iyō [iru] ga* "no matter where they may live" • *isogu koto wa aru* "they will sometimes be in a hurry" • *sō iu toki ni wa* "at such times" • *dare ga nan to iō [iu] to* "no matter what anyone may say" • *michi wa nagaku, sekai wa hiroku kanjirareru [kanjiru]* "we feel the road to be long and the world to be wide" • *mochiron* "of course" •

❖ *Yamanote-sen*: the line that circles Tokyo in a loop; it has 29 stations. ❖ *nokke kara*: "from the start," connoting "without warning." ❖ *sore kara*: a set phrase; "and then; in addition." ❖ *ikan*: =*ikenai*. ❖ *doko ni sunde iyō*: stem + *~ō/yō* = no matter *~*.

---

kuruma ga muyō no supīdo o dasu koto ni wa "as for cars speeding unnecessarily" • *boku mo hantai da keredo* "I also am against it, but" • *da kara to itte [iu]* "nevertheless" • *kō iu kimyō na gengo-kankaku no kanban o* "billboards with this kind of strange language (lit., 'verbal sensibility')" • *seken ni makichirashite [makichirasu] ii mono darō ka?* "is it a good thing to spew (lit., 'scatter') them all over the world?" • *kono te no osekkai-kanban wa* "as for this brand of officious billboard" • *keisatsu-kankei ga ichiban ōi yō ni omou* "it seems to me the majority of them are police-related" • *sono hotondo wa* "almost all of them"

妙で、しかも役に立たない。　僕は一度山梨あたりで「スピード出すな、死んでしまえばもうおしまい」というのを見たことがあるけれど、こういうのを見ているとだんだん情けなくなってくる。　気持が沈んでくる。　あるいはそれが日本の官僚組織の本質なのかもしれないけれど、お節介な上にどうしようもなく下品である。　世間のドライヴァーがこんな標語を目にとめてそれでスピードを緩めるとはとても僕には思えない。　無視するか、あるいは笑いとばすのが落ちだろう。　それにもともと底の浅いごろあわせみたいな文句だから、何度も見ているうちに見る方は何も感じなくなってくる。　そうなると、あとはもうただうるさく感じるだけだ。　日本の警察の広報というのは言語感覚が極度に遅れている上に、何となく

- *sukuiyō [sukū + yō] ga naku [nai] kimyō de [de aru]* "are hopelessly (lit., 'beyond rescue') strange" • *shikamo* "moreover" • *yaku ni tatanai [tatsu]* "they serve no purpose" • *ichido* "once" • *Yamanashi [ken] atari de* "somewhere around Yamanashi [Prefecture]" • *"Supīdo dasu na, shinde [shinu] shimaeba [shimau] oshimai"* "'Don't speed—it's all over once you've gone and died'" • *~ to iu no o mita [miru] koto ga aru keredo* "I once saw one saying ~ , but" • *kō iu no o mite iru to* "when you see something like this" • *dandan nasakenaku [nasakenai] natte kuru* "one slowly starts to feel wretched" • *kimochi ga shizunde [shizumu] kuru* "one's gets low-spirited (lit., 'the spirit sinks')" • *aruiwa* "possibly" • *sore ga Nihon no kanryō-soshiki no honshitsu na no ka mo shirenai* "that might be the essence of Japanese bureaucratism (lit., 'bureaucratic organization')" • *keredo* "but" • *osekkai na ue ni* "besides being officious" • *dō shiyō mo naku gehin de aru* "it is irretrievably vulgar" • *seken no doraibā ga* "the drivers of the world" • *konna hyōgo o me ni tomete [tomeru]* "they will spot this slogan, and" • *sore de supīdo o yurumeru* "they will then reduce their speed" • *~ to wa totemo boku ni wa omoenai* "I just don't think (lit., 'can't think') that ~ (i.e., it just doesn't seem likely to me)" • *mushi suru ka* "they will ignore it or" • *aruiwa waraitobasu no ga* "or they will dismiss it with a laugh" • *~ ochi darō* "that will no

❖ *aruiwa*: usually means "or; or else," but here "maybe; possibly." ❖ *dō shiyō mo naku*: *dō shiyō mo nai* ("there is no way to do"): hopelessly, terribly; *shiyō* = *yarikata, hōhō* (方法); *dō shiyō mo nai hito* "a hopeless case." ❖ *totemo boku ni wa omoenai*: *totemo* here intensifies the verb; for *omoenai*. ❖ *ochi darō*: *ochi* usually refers to an outcome with slightly negative connotations; also the punch line of a joke or story. ❖ *mite iru uchi ni*: ~ *uchi ni* = while ~ing, in the course of ~ing. ❖ *urusaku kanjiru*: *urusai* refers to something annoying or obtrusive as well as physically noisy. ❖ *okurete iru*: *okureru*, usually "to be late," but here "backward; behind the times."

doubt be the upshot of it" • *sore ni* "in addition (to that)" • *motomoto* "at base" • *soko no asai goroawase mitai na monku da kara* "since it is a phrase like a weak (lit., 'shallow') play on words" • *nando mo mite iru uchi ni* "in the course of seeing it many times" • *miru hō wa nani mo kanjinaku natte kuru* "those who see it become numb to it (lit., 'come not to feel anything')" • *sō naru to* "once that happens" • *ato wa* "what remains" • *mō tada urusaku kanjiru dake da* "really, one only feels it is annoying" • *Nihon no keisatsu no kōhō to iu no wa* "the public relations (activities) of the police in Japan" • *gengo-kankaku ga kyokutan ni okurete [okureru] iru ue ni* "besides being extremely backward in their sense of language" • *nan to naku* "somehow or other"

上意下達という感がある。

あるいは僕はどうでもいいようなことに対して、いちいち文句を言いすぎているのかもしれない。でもちょっと考えてみてほしい。ある日、日本国中から今ある標語ポスターとか看板とかを一枚残らず取り去って海に捨てちゃったとしてもたぶん誰も困らないですよ。絶対に。犯罪だって、事故だって、いじめだって、選挙の棄権だって、汚職だって、強姦だって、アル中だって、覚醒剤だって、標語があって減るものじゃないし、逆になくなって増えるものでもない。はっきり言えば、そんなものの大半はまったく無益・無用のものなのだ。それは情報ですらないのだ。じゃあどうしてそんなものが必要なのですか？　我々にはもっと必要な情報があるはずであ

• *jōi-katatsu to iu kan ga aru* "have a whiff of being messages delivered from the rulers to the ruled" • *aruiwa* "possibly; or else" • *dō de mo ii yō na koto ni taishite* "concerning something that doesn't make any difference" • *ichi-ichi monku o iisugite [iu + sugiru] iru no ka mo shirenai* "I might be complaining too much over this and that" • *de mo* "but" • *chotto kangaete [kangaeru] mite hoshii* "I would like (you) to think about it a little" • *aru hi* "one day" • *Nihon kokujū kara* "from throughout Japan" • *ima aru hyōgo posutā to ka kanban to ka o* "the posters or billboards with slogans which we have now" • *ichimai nokorazu [=nokoranaide] torisatte [torisaru] umi ni sutechatta [=sutete shimatta] to shite mo* "even if one removed every single one of them (lit., 'without a single one left') and threw them in the sea" • *tabun* "probably" • *dare mo komaranai [komaru] desu yo* "no one would be troubled" • *zettai ni* "absolutely (no one would be troubled)" • *hanzai datte* "even crime" • *jiko datte* "even accidents" • *ijime datte* "even bullying among students" • *senkyo no kiken datte* "even failing to vote in elections" • *oshoku datte* "even corruption" • *gōkan datte* "even rape" • *aruchū [arukōru chūdoku] datte* "even alcoholism" • *kakusei-zai datte* "even drugs (lit., 'stimulants')" • *hyōgo ga atte [aru] heru mono ja nai shi* "they won't decrease just because there are slogans, and" • *gyaku ni nakunatte [nakunaru]*

❖ *dō de mo ii yō na koto*: a trifle, an unimportant matter. ❖ *zettai ni*: an example of inversion for effect; the phrase modifies the preceding *komaranai*. ❖ *ijime*: bullying among younger students (sometimes resulting in death) is currently a major problem in Japan. ❖ *sura*: generally equivalent to *sae* (even), but narrower in usage and most often accompanying a negative verb; note that *sura* comes between *de* and *aru* (the verb *de aru*).

---

fueru mono de mo nai "neither would they increase if there were no more (billboards)" • *hakkiri ieba [iu]* "frankly speaking" • *sonna mono no taihan wa* "the majority of such things" • *mattaku mueki-muyō no mono na no da* "they are completely futile and useless" • *sore wa jōhō de sura nai no da* "they aren't even informative" • *jā* "well" • *dōshite sonna mono ga hitsuyō na no desu ka?* "why is it necessary to have such things?" • *wareware ni wa* "for us" • *motto hitsuyō na jōhō ga aru hazu de aru* "there must be information that is more necessary (than that)"

る。あんなに何の役にも立たない標語を作ったり貼ったりする暇があるのなら、どうしてもっと正確で見やすい道路標識とか住居表示を町に充実させないのだろうと思う。腹を立てているわけではない。これは本当に純粋な疑問なのだ。

僕が逆に今いちばん標語を貼ってみたいと思っている場所はラブ・ホテルの部屋の中。

「本当にそんなことをしなくちゃいけないんですか?」とか、「終わると虚しいでしょう?」とか、「だいたいいつも同じではありませんか?」とか、そういうお節介な標語をいっぱい書いて貼ってみたい。ほとんど嫌がらせで。

• *anna ni nan no yaku ni mo tatanai [tatsu] hyōgo o* "such good-for-nothing slogans (lit., 'such slogans that serve no purpose whatsoever')" • *tsukuttari [tsukuru] hattari [haru] suru hima ga aru no nara* "if (officials) have the spare time to make and put up (lit., 'paste up') ~ " • *dōshite ~ machi ni jūjitsu sasenai [suru] no darō* "why don't they improve (lit. 'enrich; make more complete') the towns by ~ ?" • *motto seikaku de [de aru] miyasui [miru + yasui] dōro hyōshiki to ka jūsho hyōji o* "more exact and easy-to-read road signs or notices for addresses" • *~ to omou* "that's what I think" • *hara o tatete [tateru] iru wake de wa nai* "it's not that I'm angry" • *kore wa hontō ni junsui na gimon na no da* "this is simply a doubt" • *boku ga gyaku ni ima ichiban hyōgo o hatte [haru] mitai to omotte [omou] iru basho wa* "the place where, on the contrary (i.e., on the other hand), I would now most like to put up slogans" • *rabu-hoteru no heya no naka* "(that is) inside the rooms of a 'love hotel'" • *"Hontō ni sonna koto o shinakucha [shinakute wa] ikenai n' desu ka?" to ka* "'Do you really have to do that?'" or" • *"Owaru to munashii deshō?' to ka* "or 'Don't you feel empty when it's over?'" • *"Daitai itsumo onaji de wa arimasen ka?" to ka* "or 'Isn't it always about the same?'" • *sō iu osekkai na hyōgo o* "such officious slogans" • *ippai kaite [kaku] hatte [haru] mitai* "I'd like to write and put up lots of

❖ *hyōgo o tsukuttari hattari suru*:~*tari* ~ ~*tari suru* = "doing things like ~." ❖ *hara o tatete iru*: to be angry (lit., "one's stomach stands up"); also *hara ga tatsu*. ❖ *rabu-hoteru*: special hotels (sometimes lavishly decorated) for rent by the hour, responding to the needs of single people who live with their parents until marriage and married couples who have little privacy from children or cohabiting parents. ❖ *iyagarase*: something done out of spite or to annoy someone; somewhat stronger than *itazura*.

them" • *hotondo iyagarase de* "just to be nasty; just for the hell of it"

Japanese, a fact brought home to me when I returned to the study of French after a few years in Japan. It is only after studying Japanese that one appreciates how close English is to European languages in vocabulary, sentence construction, and way of thinking. Of course, that's exactly what makes Japanese so fascinating as well as so frustrating.

At any rate, the Japanese essays reproduced here are exactly as originally published, with no abridgment or revision. For convenience of use, the vocabulary list and notes are found on the same page as the Japanese text or on the facing page. The vocabulary list, which incorporates readings for all *kanji*, is arranged by phrase. I hope that this will guide students away from word-by-word translations and also help them in deconstructing the more complicated sentences found in the later pieces.

In the notes I have attempted to explain special usages and point out frequently used rhetorical devices, transitional words, and idiomatic usages, but it was of course impossible to explain everything. Indeed, preparing the notes impressed upon me the importance of wide reading and other exposure to "real" Japanese in movies, television, and the like, where one can learn idioms and turns of phrase in context—and the particular difficulty of seemingly easy words such as *are*, *sore*, *mō*, *nani*, *mono*, and *totemo*. Readers will also notice that punctuation in general and the use of *katakana* to give a certain degree of emphasis (similar to italics or quotation marks in English) seem to be little standardized and to differ widely from author to author.

Happy reading!

*

I would like to take this opportunity to thank my various Japanese teachers, including Mr. Susumu Nagara at the University of Michigan, Mr. Akira Miura at the University of Wisconsin, and Mrs. Nobuko Mizutani and the other teachers of the Inter-University Center for Japanese Studies (then in Tokyo and now in Yokohama).

More particularly I would like gratefully to acknowledge the assistance of Mr. Michael Brase and Mr. Shigeyoshi Suzuki at Kodansha International, especially in the preparation of the notes.

Preface

In this reader of contemporary Japanese essays, I have tried to help readers overcome the problems I myself experienced as a student of Japanese. The first is one of selection, deciding what to read once one has a basic grounding in Japanese grammar and has learned several hundred *kanji*.

I myself tried reading what I thought would be easiest, the newspaper and mysteries. However, I now realize that newspapers are fairly difficult in their condensed style and high frequency of *kanji* compound words, and that mystery fiction is hard because of its highly colloquial language with contractions and idiomatic usages not taught in the classroom. I have found that nonfiction for a general reader, as in the essays collected together here, is easiest.

I also hope that the essays here, roughly arranged in increasing level of difficulty, will be *interesting* to foreign readers, both intrinsically and as a glimpse into the attitudes and thinking of a younger generation of writers few of whom are well known in the West. Reading texts presently available for students of Japanese tend to fall into two categories: those which unconsciously (I hope!) view the student as a child who needs to be socialized into Japanese culture by reading fairy tales and learning about Japanese festivals and other traditional customs (the Momotaro school) or, on the other hand, those which treat the learner as a budding Japan Studies scholar eager to read about Buddhism, feudalism, classical literature, and the like (the Fukuzawa Yukichi school).

Hopefully the pieces here, in a variety of styles and voices, will be of interest to a wide range of readers, and the vocabulary lists and notes will make them accessible to learners at various levels in their studies. I well remember how discouraging it was not to be able to read freely in Japanese even after three or four years of study at an American university, especially after having been able to read plays and novels in my second-year German class.

I used to think that this was solely a *kanji* problem, but later realized that a limited vocabulary and knowledge of idioms was equally to blame. One literally starts from zero when ones learn

Contents

Preface vii

Mori Yōko 3
 逃がした魚は大きかった

Sakamoto Ryūichi 17
 友よ、また逢おう

Tawara Machi 29
 心に届く言葉

Nejime Shōichi 39
 昼寝をしている私の直木賞百万円

Sakura Momoko 59
 宴会用の女

Itō Seikō 93
 天安門事件のこと

Yoshimoto Banana 111
 幸福の瞬間

Murakami Haruki 133
 「狭い日本・明るい家庭」

Distributed in the United States by Kodansha America, Inc., 114 Fifth Avenue, New York New York 10011, and in the United Kingdom and continental Europe by Kodansha Europe, Ltd., 95 Aldwych, London WC2B 4JF. Published by Kodansha International, Ltd., 17-14 Otowa 1-chome, Bunkyo-ku, Tokyo 112, and Kodansha America, Inc.

First edition 1994
94 95 96 10 9 8 7 6 5 4 3 2 1

ISBN 4-7700-1754-5

READ REAL JAPANESE

Janet Ashby

KODANSHA INTERNATIONAL
Tokyo · New York · London